My friend and colleague  absolute change to m' where he brings the d mind of God to the "main street" mind-set of the average person. When Bishop Grillo speaks of God's insatiable desire to bless us with such favor, I am overwhelmed that a holy God considers me with such jealous detail.

—BISHOP MANWELL GRADY
THE POTTER'S HOUSE MINISTRIES OF N.C.
REIDSVILLE, NORTH CAROLINA

Have you ever met anyone for the first time, and it seemed like you have been joined together for a lifetime? That expresses the relationship that Bishop Jerry Grillo and I share. Bishop Grillo is a major voice on the horizon today speaking with much clarity, conviction and consistency on God's favor. God is using him in ministry from coast to coast. He preaches and teaches daily by way of his books and personal appearances. As you journey through the pages of this book on the favor of God, you will grow spiritually and have a great appreciation of God's favor. Bishop Grillo is indeed one of God's mouthpieces for this hour. His writing is as powerful, profound and prolific as his preaching. You cannot read this book without changing the way you think. Hopefully, you will have a change of heart.

—BISHOP ROBERT F. HARGROVE II
"THE CATHEDRAL" G.R.A.C.E. FAMILY CHURCH
ATLANTIC CITY, NEW JERSEY

It is not often we find Spirit-filled books of faith. Bishop Grillo is anointed to reach all ages. He is humble, and his love for people is exposed through everything joined to his ministry. I am blessed to know this man of God. Everyone with whom I have shared his books says he was (speaking) directly to them. Their lives were changed immediately.

—Bishop Charles R. Lyles
Victory First Presbyterian
Deliverance Church
Atlantic City, New Jersey

When it comes to supernatural favor and prosperity, God has given Bishop Grillo wisdom and an anointing to transfer that knowledge through the revelation of God's Word. I can only pray that everyone will be afforded the opportunity I have been given. The truths found in this book will change your life forever...it has mine.

—Pastor Vincent Fields
Greater Works Ministries
Atlantic City, New Jersey

Bishop Jerry Grillo is a fresh new voice for the body of Christ to reach this generation with the revelation of God's favor and increase. He is a great example of what God can do with people who have made themselves available to be used by him.

—Pastor Jeff Poole
New Hope Church of God
Kathleen, Georgia

Bishop Jerry Grillo is truly a gift from God to my life. I love his passion, his purity and his painstaking commitment to purpose. It is very obvious that he loves the God he writes to us about. Should you ever have the privilege of peaking into the favor on his life, you would know without a doubt he's one of God's favorite kids. Bishop Jerry Grillo—what a wonderful refreshing, what a wonderful friend!

—Pastor Sheryl Brady
The River & Sheryl Brady Ministries
Raleigh, North Carolina

Pastor Richie,
Get ready for supernatural
Favor

FAVOR
MAKES NO SENSE

JERRY A. GRILLO JR.

CREATION
HOUSE PRESS
A STRANG COMPANY

FAVOR MAKES NO SENSE by Bishop Jerry A. Grillo Jr.
Published by Creation House Press
A Strang Company
600 Rinehart Road
Lake Mary, FL 32746
www.creationhouse.com

Unless otherwise noted, all Scripture quotations are from the Holy Bible, New International Version. Copyright © 1973, 1978, 1984, International Bible Society. Used by permission.

Scripture quotations marked AMP are from the Amplified Bible. Old Testament copyright © 1965, 1987 by the Zondervan Corporation. The Amplified New Testament copyright © 1954, 1958, 1987 by the Lockman Foundation. Used by permission.

Scripture quotations marked KJV are from the King James Version of the Bible.

Scripture quotations marked NKJV are from the New King James Version of the Bible. Copyright © 1979, 1980, 1982 by Thomas Nelson, Inc., publishers. Used by permission.

Cover design by Larry Smith & Associates
Interior design by David Bilby

Library of Congress Control Number: 2003106692
International Standard Book Number: 1-59185-239-0

03 04 05 06 07 — 9 8 7 6 5 4 3 2 1
Printed in the United States of America

I want to dedicate this book to the one person I can say has believed in me and stuck with me...when I know she shouldn't have.

This person has been to me the strength that causes you to push on when everything in you is saying give up. She has preached me out of heartaches; she has pulled me out of crisis and loved me in spite of!

Maryann, I dedicate not only this manuscript to you but also my life to you...you are a wonderful friend, companion and a wonderful mother to our children, Jerry and Jordan.

I love you and respect your anointing to carry on with the promises of God.

I also want to say to my children, Jerry and Jordan, that you are a source of joy and sunshine to me. Daddy loves you dearly.

CONTENTS

Favor is not what you wear; favor is what you are.

—JERRY A. GRILLO JR.

For you, O Lord, will bless the righteous; with favor You will surround him as with a shield.

—PSALM 5:12, NKJV

FOREWORD

This book could be the turning point of your faith life.

The Person of Jesus creates your peace.

The Principles of Jesus create your prosperity.

That is why the uncommon wisdom in these pages is so very important to your personal success. You will learn how your *words* are the gates to the future you are pursuing and how to apply the laws of favor that unleash the miracles you have been waiting for your entire lifetime.

Bishop Jerry Grillo lives what he teaches. It has been my privilege to be his personal friend for a number of years. He is a living example of a victorious and happy leader. His church is a victorious church. His lovely wife and children reflect the glorious presence of God and the understanding of the laws of God. His revelation is like fresh air in a stagnant world. He is one of the happiest and most exciting leaders I have known throughout my thirty-seven years of world evangelism.

It is a privilege to commend this book to every person who treasures excellence, success and uncommon victories.

Read it carefully and often. Mark it with your highlighter. Use it as a daily devotional at your family breakfast table. Your pursuit of this wisdom will not go unrewarded.

—MIKE MURDOCK, PH.D.

A WORD FROM BISHOP GRILLO

We have had our revivals in times past. The faith movement, the salvation movement, the name-it-claim-it movement, the prophecy movement and many others.

I believe that we are about to walk into a revival of the *favor of God*, and when favor comes, it will absolutely make no sense. The greatest gift God gave us is favor!

Favor is the mercies of God personified.

Favor is the umbilical cord to what God has for us.

Favor will be the ingredient that will cause us to fulfill our destiny.

Favor is something that we are allowed to walk in. Everyone has the potential to walk in the favor of God.

Favor is a decision! Salvation is free...everything else will require something on your part. Everyone wants favor; however, not everyone is willing to do what it takes to obtain favor.

Favor will make the devil pay!

Favor will cause you to walk in circles you aren't qualified to be in.

Favor is the transfer of access.

Favor will have you driving a new car and someone else making the payment.

Money can't buy you favor...but favor can get you money.

Favor can change your medical report.

Favor will postpone the storm that was scheduled to destroy you.

Favor will promote you while others are trying to destroy you.

Favor will protect you.

Caution

When we are seeking the Lord we need to be aware that we should seek the Lord for who He is and not for what He can do for us. I'm a firm believer in the law of expectancy, and I believe that we need to expect the Lord to bless us. However, when I seek the Lord, I am not looking for His mighty acts; I'm looking for His mighty hand of love, mercy and presence. In this we will find His hand of favor.

Let me put it in this terminology. Seek the Lord's left hand of holiness, and you will receive His right hand of favor.

For five years I have been teaching and preaching on favor. I can honestly say that when you walk according to the precepts and bylaws of the Word of God, you will begin to experience awesome favor. My first book on favor was titled *The Weather Forecast for Your Future... Extreme F.O.G.* In that book I wrote about what it means to walk in the F.O.G. (favor of God), how to become the F.O.G. and so forth.

THE ANATOMY OF FAVOR

According to Webster's dictionary, *anatomy* is defined as the structure of an organism or body. That's what I want to do in the first part of this book. I want to build the structure and the body of favor.

It will be my challenge and desire to answer questions such as, What is favor? How do we receive it? Can anyone have it?

> *One day of favor is worth a*
> *thousand days of labor!*
> —DR. MIKE MURDOCK

INTRODUCTION

E very generation has a period in which they speculate if what they have heard about the stories of God in past generations is true.

It seems that with the growing of our society and its technology there is little, if any, interest in godly principles. The church as we know it is going through dramatic and uncomfortable change. This change is occurring in every area of the churches' ministries from the nursery to the pulpit—changes such as the music, the attitude of the people, the questions of our youth and people's opinion of how a church service ought to be. Our old way of doing things seems to be losing its appeal to this twenty-first-century generation.

Although change can be uncomfortable, I believe it is necessary. People are looking for the Spirit of the Lord. They want more than just someone standing in the pulpit and teaching about what God did in times past. This new generation is asking the question, "If there is a living God, where is He?" This is a great question. When people start asking and looking for God, they begin to ignite in themselves the passion and desire to pursue the answer. I believe the Bible refers to it as "seeking."

When people start seeking for the Spirit of God, they begin to look, ask and seek for what will cause God to respond to them. In times past, people would become curious about the Spirit of the Lord before every move of God. People became tired of just religion and started looking for the God of heaven and earth.

The Word of God says that if we seek Him we are going to most likely find Him. When we find God, we find:

- His goodness
- His mercy
- His presence
- His power
- His love

God is not hiding from us; He is not avoiding us. He wants us to know Him and to know the power of His resurrection. However, to know God in His power, we must be willing to fellowship in His sufferings. We all want the blessings, but not all of us are willing to do what it takes to receive the blessings!

This book is written just for that reason—to explain and build a passion for those in the body of Christ so they can grow up and walk in the favor of God. When favor comes, it will make no sense.

As believers, God wants to expose us to the fullness of His power. We are all His children and have inherited rights by adoption. However, God is not going to release all His fullness until we are ready and capable of handling them correctly.

In all that God has for us, we must first understand the fundamentals of the walk of God and then move into the depth of God.

We call this growing up! Growth is the ability to adjust, the ability to look at situations differently than when we were children. Children look at things differently than adults. Children can only see what the immediate problem or desire is, but an adult sees the big picture.

I have two children. They absolutely go nuts when I say *no* to a certain toy they want. They act and look as if the whole world has come to an end. Now, we as adults should have a whole different perspective on life when we don't get what we want. We realize that life sometimes has a waiting process before we can have what we desire. So we just go on with a whole different viewpoint.

> When I was a child, I talked like a child, I thought like a child, I reasoned like a child. When I became a man, I put childish ways behind me.
> —1 CORINTHIANS 13:11

God is not hiding from His children!

Life is a process! That's all, nothing more and nothing less.

Dr. John Maxwell says that success is not a destination; success is a journey. Well, so is life! Life is made up of good days and bad days, sick days and healthy days. I have often said that people put too much emphasis on Satan and about what happens to us on a daily basis. The truth is that life is full of ups and downs. When we make peace with this understanding, we are going to free ourselves of all kinds of headaches and stress.

Life is living and fulfilling our daily process to our destiny.

Process is living and accepting the changes that occur through our struggles and victories. If we happen to mess up today, process is for us to get up tomorrow and work at not messing up. This is what separates us from the animal kingdom—the ability to make our own changes without anyone telling us we have to change. Thus we are in the process to the next level of promotion or blessing.

CHAPTER 1

PROCESS, THE FIRST KEY TO COMPLETE VICTORY!

O ne of the greatest things to me in the Bible is the first chapter of the Book of Genesis. In the first encounter of God and His immense power we see that, instead of taking just moments to create the world in which we live, He took six days.

God could have spoken everything into existence with one word. God chose to take His time and walk through the process of building and enjoying what He was doing on the way to completion. This has caused me to ask the question, "Why God? Why did you do it in the process of time?"

The answer I came up with was that God was trying to teach us through the interpretation of the Word that we are not going to complete everything in life in one day.

God took six days to create what He could have created with one word. God was comfortable with completing a day of work and looking at what He had created, and even though nothing was entirely in its place, God saw that it was "good."

We need to evaluate life in the same manner. When

you look at yourself, take into consideration that it takes time for change to manifest. We may not be complete or perfect, but we are working on it through the power of the Word of God. God is patient; people are not. God's mercy allows Him the ability to wait on us to gain control of ourselves.

> Being confident of this, that he who began a good work in you will carry it on to completion until the day of Christ Jesus.
>
> —PHILIPPIANS 1:6

THE GREAT FALLING AWAY!

Have you noticed that in the past years a lot of people seem to be coming to the Lord? There are numerous amounts of people turning in what we call conversion cards—with our "seeker friendly" mentality and the "heaven and hell" dramas—yet where are all these people? In my hometown a church put on a drama about heaven and hell. They boasted that over seven hundred people received Christ as their personal Savior. That church's average attendance was around two hundred, and today it is still around the same size. Now let me ask you a question: If seven hundred people received Christ, wouldn't you think that that church would have at least grown in size to more than two hundred people? *Something's missing!*

We had a crusade in our city, and at the end of this crusade they boasted about thirty thousand people who came. This was the biggest crowd of people coming to a crusade in the history of my city. Now, again let me ask you a question: Where are all those people? Not one church seemed to have grown to a noticeable difference.

Church has become a place of watered-down principles. We have made it too easy to say *yes* and too difficult for anyone to line up with our standards. People need to be taught that they are not going to walk right out of their problems just because they confess Jesus as Lord. The falling away is the result of crowd-pleasing; it is not a covenant teaching.

It has become too easy to get saved. People used to feel convicted in a church service. Now they are entertained to the point where they just decide to give this Christianity a try. They leave our crusades, and there is no one teaching the process of being saved. Our "masses" mentality has caused us to lose heart for "neighbor" mentality.

Salvation is instant and progressive. When we accept Christ in our hearts, we have instantly gained access to God, and that access allows us the ability to start the changing process of spiritual growth. The one glitch in having a life completely free from sin is *flesh!* The spirit of a man is saved, but the mind must be renewed daily.

The first key to favor is nonconformity. We as believers will only gain a level of freedom from what we used to live in—worry, fear, anger, sexual sins or anything that was keeping us from the hand of God's favor—when we make a choice to conform to the Word of God instead of our flesh.

> Do not conform any longer to the pattern of this world, but be transformed by the renewing of your mind. Then you will be able to test and approve what God's will is—his good, pleasing and perfect will.
>
> —ROMANS 12:2

Favor occurs when we make up our minds to quit following after the patterns of this world and start developing new patterns that are formed by the renewing of our minds through the Word of God. To be highly favored we can't be like everyone; we must be what God wants us to be.

CHAPTER 2

YOU ARE
HİGHLY FAVORED!

O f all the women that were living in the Middle East during the time of the birth of Jesus, why did God choose Mary? Why did He profess her to be highly favored? I believe that the answer we are seeking is in this phrase, "The Lord is with you."

> In the sixth month, God sent the angel Gabriel to Nazareth, a town in Galilee, to a virgin pledged to be married to a man named Joseph, a descendant of David. The virgin's name was Mary. The angel went to her and said, "Greetings, you who are highly favored! The Lord is with you."
>
> —LUKE 1:26–28

Mary was chosen because she was a person who had already been pleasing the Lord. She was obviously more concerned about what God desired than what she desired. She was faithful with her daily lifestyle. What we do daily really determines what we are becoming.

In this the angel Gabriel called Mary highly favored.

THE COST

Mary was chosen and favored because God knew she

4

would be willing to be inconvenienced to fulfill His purpose. Anytime favor is coming, it will first require total surrender from you. Never believe for a moment that the first stage of blessing will be anything but hard. God will never pour out His hand of favor without first testing the vessel. Mary was willing to take the test, and God knew she would pass. Favor starts with the willingness to empty the vessel so it can be filled. Mary was willing to take on the embarrassment of the people. Her willingness to become pregnant while unwed would cost her massive scars to her reputation.

Think about this: Mary's culture was not as forgiving as our culture. When a woman conceived, she had better be married or she would become guilty of sin and be stoned to death for having sexual relations outside the sanctity of marriage. Mary was willing to take all this onto herself without knowing the outcome. She was willing to do whatever it took to fulfill the plans and purpose of God. Can't you see why she was chosen? Most church people today will not even give up a good night's sleep for the plans of God. Most people in our churches today have the mentality that God is OK as long as He doesn't start requiring more than they are willing to give. God is OK as long as He stays in heaven and doesn't ask of us anything that will cost our time. Not Mary. She had a whole different set of values; she was willing to be used to be favored.

I believe that angels know who is favored by God and, in return, want to be around those who have been noticed by Him. Favor is nothing more than the Lord noticing you and your faithfulness to obey Him when He is in need of you.

Favor is not what you wear...favor is what you are.

God was not going to put favor *on* Mary; He was about

to put favor *in* Mary. She was going to be filled with the seed of God. Favor was not what she was going to wear, but what she was going to be filled with.

To be highly favored you must be willing to be uncomfortable for a season. Recognize that when favor begins, it usually begins with a sacrifice on your part.

- Abraham had to offer Isaac.
- Joseph was thrown in the pit.
- Moses was cast away from his people.
- Noah had to build an ark.
- Jesus had to carry His cross.

Favor will cost up front. When favor begins to produce its fruits, you will be so blessed. Your blessings will overtake you. Favor will make no sense when it produces its fruit.

> And blessed is she that believed: for there shall be a performance of those things which were told her from the Lord. And Mary said, My soul doth magnify the Lord, and my spirit hath rejoiced in God my Saviour. For he hath regarded the low estate of his handmaiden: for, behold, from henceforth all generations shall call me blessed.
>
> —Luke 1:45–48, kjv

God was able to perform those things in which she believed. Mary's miracle and her harvest were connected to her belief system. God's level of performance was determined by the level of Mary's ability to believe all that was spoken to her by the angel of the Lord.

Favor comes to us when we are able to accept the words of the Lord without hesitation. *Hesitation is disobedience!* We should obey the moment the Lord impresses on us to do something. The instant we start thinking and questioning the reasons for what the Lord is impressing on us to do, our actions start to change. We start trying to explain away our actions instead of walking in pure faith, and in return we are costing ourselves *favor*.

We must be willing to respond at a moment's notice to be highly favored. We have the heart of instant faith. When the Lord impresses on us to sow or to do, we must quickly obey. It's that willingness to respond quickly that causes favor to flow in great quantity. Remember, when God is asking for a seed, His mind is not on our seed at that moment; it is on our harvest. God is requiring the seed that will be proportionate to our harvest.

The Benefit

Favor is a seed before it can be a harvest. You must learn to sow favor before you will be able to reap favor.

God performed everything that was told to Mary at the level that she believed. Walking in obedience to the level of your faith is an incredible truth and understanding.

I was sitting in my office one Friday afternoon when I heard that still small voice in my heart tell me to go to a certain furniture store, and take my youth pastor and my praise and worship pastor with me. I was very busy finalizing plans for our upcoming conference and really felt that I needed to stay at the office; however, I knew that I could feel the nudge of the Spirit, so I obeyed.

When we walked into that store, I knew that the Lord had gone before me. The store owner saw me and immediately said, "Bishop, the last time you visited us our store wasn't doing well in sales. After you left, our sales doubled." She then proceeded to walk to her office and came out holding a brand-new $100 bill, which she said she had been holding for me since the last time I was there.

In the meantime, Holli, my praise and worship pastor,

was admiring a statue. When the owner noticed that she
liked it, she immediately sowed it into her life. Now we
both walked out blessed.

While riding down the road, I heard the Holy Spirit
say, "How would you like to know where money is waiting on you every day? I can show you where your blessings are daily! Just walk in hourly obedience."

How about it? Wouldn't you love to know every day
where God is hiding your blessing? You can! It's called
walking in *favor*!

We have been highly favored. You should stop right
now and begin to praise and worship the Lord and thank
Him for His hand of favor. After all, if it hadn't been for
the Lord who was on our side, we would have all died on
the journey to greatness. Amen?

CHAPTER 3

YOU ARE FAVORED WHEN GOD NOTICES YOU!

The first key to success in this world is to attract the look of God. Favor comes to us when we have attracted God.

FAVOR KEY #1: FAVOR COMES WHEN THE RIGHT ONE NOTICES YOU.

You don't have to be noticed by everyone; however, you do have to be noticed by the right one. The individual noticing you must be in a place or position that can make the golden connection for you. Everybody needs a Jonathan connection. David may have killed Goliath, which gave him the access he needed to get in the palace, but it was Jonathan, Saul's son, that noticed him and made the connection with David to keep him in the palace. A lot of men have been invited to the palace; however, there's no accomplishment in being invited to the palace. The accomplishment is when you can stay in the palace, and to do that you will need someone to notice you and teach you palace protocol; you'll need a Jonathan connection!

Great men and women with the gift of discernment will recognize those who have been favored and those who have the potential to do great things. They will want to put their time and energy into helping you understand palace protocol when they sense you are favored.

I was at a restaurant standing at the salad bar when a man of God who was standing beside me said, "The question for you is not 'Are you?' The question for you is 'When are you?'" It's not that you haven't been chosen or that the hand of greatness is not upon you, but when are you going to do what God has predestined for you?" The man of God *noticed the hand of favor on me*. When great men or women sense the hand of favor on you, they want to help make the connection.

Here's where I love the law of favor. It makes no sense that this preacher would desire to hook up with me when his ministry triples mine in size and influence. His church alone runs over twenty-four hundred people. When favor hits, it makes no sense.

> He looketh on the earth, and it trembleth: he toucheth the hills, and they smoke.
> —PSALM 104:32, KJV

Just one look from the Lord, and the earth around you will tremble. Having the man of God notice me was my look from the Lord. One look and whatever was holding you will let go. Your struggles, whatever's been holding you down or keeping you in bondage, will tremble at just one look from God.

FAVOR KEY #2: YOU MUST BE ABLE TO NOTICE THE RIGHT MAN.

We must develop the ability to recognize and notice

greatness in others—learning to discern who has been favored and is in a position to increase you. Let me caution you, these men are put into your life to increase you in their knowledge and wisdom, *not their wealth.*

The most dangerous thing to do when you enter the atmosphere of great men or women is to begin to build a mind-set that they are going to give you what they have. Great men and women want to mentor, not become your financial source. There is only one source, and that is God.

Learn to be a servant. Learn to listen and be a support to them. In due season you will benefit by their noticing you, and you will receive favor when they do. All you need is recognition from these men, and you will be on your way to destiny. Elisha washed the hands of Elijah, his mentor, for fifteen years before the mantle fell. Elisha served the man of God long enough for what was in Elijah to be transferred to him. He noticed who was noticing him. This is an incredible and powerful understanding. When we are able to stay put long enough, we will begin to attract God's favor.

I preached in Dallas at a Winter Wisdom Conference with Dr. Mike Murdock not long ago. While I was approaching my tape and book table, a man came up to me and asked what he could do to get into the ministry.

My response wasn't what he was looking for. I informed him that he needed to get in a church where there is a mentoring pastor. Some pastors and bishops have the call to father and mother children. These men and women of God are called to raise up sons and daughters in the ministry. Not all pastors are mentoring pastors. When you find a father, you have found a mentoring pastor. When you find that church, start serving that man of God.

"Serve the man of God?" was his reply. Absolutely.

Serve him! Carry his briefcase, get him water, find out what kind of mints he likes, and keep hot tea ready. Serve, serve, and serve! The anointing you serve will most likely be the anointing you will carry.

When your mentor believes you are ready, he will release you to your next season of promotion or ministry. Learn to wait on godly promotion. The fastest way to promotion is servanthood—serving will put you in places to be noticed. Here is where favor will find you to promote you.

I have a tape series that applies here, titled "Whatever Promotes You Must Sustain You." The meaning is clear. If self promotes you, then self has to be able to hold you in hard times, but I have bad news. Self has no ability or power to hold you in troubled times. We must all wait on godly promotion to be favored; God must be the one promoting us. We can be confident that God is able to hold us through any trial when hell's fire and storms hit.

CHAPTER 4

DO YOU HAVE THE FRAGRANCE THAT ATTRACTS HIS FAVOR?

I n the fifth chapter of John we find a great multitude—a crowd of needy people. Jesus was walking through a sea of hurting, sick, lame and blind.

> Now there is at Jerusalem by the sheep market a pool, which is called in the Hebrew tongue Bethesda, having five porches. In these lay a great multitude of impotent folk, of blind, halt, withered, waiting for the moving of the water.
>
> —JOHN 5:2–3, KJV

Doesn't it seem odd that Jesus did nothing to help ease the suffering of this crowd? He saw their problems and He heard their cries, yet He did nothing. He showed them no favor...He was searching for someone in the crowd. The crowd had not attracted Him, but someone in the crowd did. Let's do away with the myth that the masses matter more than the individual in the masses.

Favor Key #3: Our Needs Alone Will Not Attract Favor.

It's not what we need; it's our actions. It's what we do in times of need that creates the energy of favor.

The crowd was there daily. They came to the pool of Bethesda and waited, but what were they waiting on? They were waiting for the waters to move, to stir. They did nothing but just sit and wait. Sounds like most churches. They are full of people who are waiting, and no one is willing to do anything but wait.

> For an angel went down at a certain season into the pool, and troubled the water: whosoever then first after the troubling of the water stepped in was made whole of whatsoever disease he had.
>
> —John 5:4, kjv

What were these people waiting on? They were waiting for God to move. They were sitting in an area where the Spirit of the Lord would show up at certain seasons. The one thing we must all realize is that there is a season for everything. Ecclesiastes 3:1 says, "There is a time for everything. We all know the rest—a time to die, a time to live, etc. We must learn to interpret what season we are in if we want to experience favor. Certain things happen in certain seasons. Some things are unavoidable in certain seasons. For instance, if you live in the northern part of the United States, you can expect snow in winter and pollen in spring. The power to withstand times of pain is to understand what season you are in. Sometimes the greatest offense is a good defense. You must learn to hang on until favor shows up. You must learn to recognize timing if you want to walk in favor! Don't just sit down and wait; do something while you wait. Praise while you wait, study while you wait, worship while you wait, and whistle while you wait. The force of favor is hinged on the ability to do something while you are waiting.

The key to a miracle is understanding that whosoever can get whatsoever they came to receive. Favor is hinged on your moving, not waiting.

> And a certain man was there, which had infirmity thirty and eight years. When Jesus saw him lie, and knew that he had been now a long time in that case, he saith unto him, Wilt thou be made whole? The impotent man answered him, Sir, I have no man, when the water is troubled, to put me into the pool: but while I am coming, another steppeth down before me.
>
> —JOHN 5:5–7, KJV

Observe that the right man—Jesus—noticed this one man. This man was different because he was coming to the waters. He wasn't just waiting; he was coming ("while I am coming...."). He knew that if he waited he would never make it close enough to get in. The others were waiting for someone to put them in.

If you're waiting on someone to bless you, you'll most likely be waiting for a long time. People who do nothing usually don't make enough upheaval for anyone to notice them. The old adage is true, "Nothing plus nothing equals nothing." That was not the case for this certain man. Anytime we see the phrase "certain man" or "certain person" in the Word of God, it is a place for you and me to put our name. "Certain man" means it could be anyone of us.

> Jesus saith unto him, Rise, take up thy bed, and walk. And immediately the man was made whole, and took up his bed, and walked: and on the same day was the Sabbath. The Jews therefore said unto him that was

cured, It is the Sabbath day: it is not lawful for thee
to carry thy bed. He answered them, He that made
me whole, the same said unto me, Take up thy bed,
and walk. Then asked they him, what man is that
which said unto thee, Take up thy bed, and walk?

—JOHN 5:8–12

FAVOR KEY #4: GOD IS NOT LOOKING FOR THE CROWD; HE'S LOOKING FOR INDIVIDUALS IN THE CROWD.

Jesus passed by so many needy people when He was
walking through Solomon's courtyard; He passed the
impotent, the blind, the halt and the withered. Looking at
this at first glance, you begin to feel that Jesus was being
a little insensitive. Here is the Son of God, full of virtue
to heal and take care of the needy, yet He just passed by
them all and walked over to one man. This one man had
what I call the fragrance that will attract His favor. Do
you have the fragrance that will attract God's favor? This
man's persistency got him noticed. The Lord isn't as
caught up in crowds as we are. He is conscious of the one
in the crowd who needs Him the most and is willing to
do whatever it takes to receive favor.

We need to notice the multitude that He passed by
when we read this passage. I believe a further study of
these people will give us a clearer picture of why Jesus
passed by them.

The first was the *impotent folks*! The word *impotent* in
the Greek means "ineffective, powerless, helpless…no
future."

Our churches are full of impotent people—people
who just come to our services to receive and never to give
back to the ministry they are receiving from. How many

people do you know right now in your local body that just come, sit, leave and never enter in to help do anything productive? They are those who are impotent. They are powerless and useless. The pastor gives and gives, but when it's time to reciprocate what has been so freely given, these people usually leave and go somewhere else to start draining another man of God!

The second kind of folks Jesus passed was *blind folks*! The word *blind* in the Greek means "not able or willing to notice, understand or judge correctly."

This second group of people will attend your church for a while and, after time, will become judgmental and critical. These people will not even take the time neces- sary to notice what they have in their local body. Instead they look for weakness in others, and when they find it, they will point out the weakness to everyone else. These are dangerous folk. They can destroy what a man of God is doing in a matter of days. They spread their poison all over the body, like venom from snakebites.

It's not that they lack the ability to notice or to change; it's just that they are not willing to notice. They come in and immediately set up roadblocks to understanding what the Lord is doing in their church. Don't let this kind of spirit live long around you. Criticism is the most conta- gious of all these diseases.

The third kind of folks were the *halt folks*! The word *halt* in the Greek means "to be uncertain, to waver or hesitate."

Hesitation is disobedience. When the Spirit of the Lord pushes you to give or to do something in your church or in your everyday life, and you hesitate, you have just disobeyed the Lord. Why do we always have to take so much time to understand what the Lord is saying? One reason is because we don't spend enough time familiariz- ing our ears to His voice. Hesitation can be the very thing that stops favor from flowing to you.

When the spirit of giving hits the congregation during an anointed service, and you feel that deep sinking feeling in your stomach to give a certain amount, an amount that you are not accustomed to giving, understand at that moment that God is behind your giving. Neither Satan nor the flesh would ever tell you to give anything that's going to promote the kingdom of God.

If your giving won't move you, it probably won't move God.

This spirit of hesitation will stop an offering service to the point that the budget that was set and believed for won't be met. We all need to sow at our level. If you can sow $100 or $1,000 and you only sow $10, in my opinion, you are slapping God in the face. Why wouldn't you want to sow the best seeds to the Lord? Don't you believe Luke 6:38?

> Give, and it will be given to you. A good measure, pressed down, shaken together and running over, will be poured into your lap. For with the measure you use, it will be measured to you.

Either Luke 6:38 is the truth or not. If any part of the Word of God isn't true, then how do we know that John 3:16 is true? The truth is that we can stand on the whole Word of God. All of God's promises are yea and amen.

The fourth kind of folks were the *withered*. The word *withered* in the Greek means "to lose vigor or freshness."

It doesn't take a rocket scientist to figure this one out. Haven't you noticed that those who have been saved for some time seem to be miserably saved? They never enter into worship anymore; they never have smiles on their faces. They always seem to have some kind of a problem, and no one can help them. When we give them the Word, all they can do is offer up to us how long they have been in church. They just sit in church all withered up...their giving, their witness, their joy and their love...just withered. They have no vigor in the walk; they've lost that once sweet smell and fragrance of freshness.

I hope that you are not one of these four. I pray that if you are, right now you would bow your head and ask the Lord to forgive you of your ignorance and then start walking with the fragrance that will attract the Lord's favor.

The Lord isn't playing favoritism when it comes to blessing you. He has set up the same standard for everyone. That standard is to be a good steward of what He has given you. If all He has given you is a great smile, then that's all He will demand from you...to use your smile for Him.

John 5:4 says that whosoever got in first was made whole of whatsoever they came for. Whosoever got whatsoever they needed. Favor is for everybody!

One man kept coming; he kept movement in his life for thirty-eight years. Why? He lacked the knowledge to know when the spirit of favor was going to stir the pool again. He couldn't take the chance that if he stayed home one day, he might miss the day that he was supposed to get his miracle.

FAVOR KEY #5: FAVOR IS SEASONAL.

For an angel went down *at a certain season* into the pool, and troubled the water: whosoever then first after the troubling of the water stepped in was made whole of whatsoever disease he had.

—JOHN 5:4, KJV, EMPHASIS ADDED

Blessings come to us through windows of opportunity. One of the greatest mistakes made in the sowing and reaping message is to expect an immediate response to a seed that has been sowed.

It takes time for favor to come. I like telling my congregation that however long it is taking your harvest to manifest is a clue to how big your harvest is. Big things take longer to set up. Don't let hopelessness and despair set in. They will cause you to dig up your seed and ruin your harvest.

Favor comes in season. Learn to wait on the Lord and watch your harvest start coming. Waiting is the proof of trust. If your blessing or harvest hasn't manifested yet, then guess what? It's on the way! Keep circumstances from shipwrecking your faith! Keep your mind on the Lord. The Word of God says that perfect peace is those minds that are stayed on Him. Just keep your focus.

Success isn't magic or hocus pocus; success is simply learning how to focus.

PERSISTENCE PAYS OFF

The fragrance that attracted Jesus was the fragrance of persistence. This man just kept coming to the water for his miracle. The lack of persistence is one of the greatest weaknesses that the church faces today. As a body, we have lost the ability to endure until God shows up and delivers us from our pain, problems and hurts.

> When Jesus saw him lie, and knew that he had been now a long time in that case, he saith unto him, Wilt thou be made whole? The impotent man answered him, Sir, I have no man, when the water is troubled, to put me into the pool: but while I am coming, another steppeth down before me.
>
> —JOHN 5:6–7, KJV

This man wasn't born into this condition. He had,

through his lifestyle, developed a sickness that had caused him to suffer for thirty-eight years. Maybe he had caught a sexually transmitted disease, which caused atrophy in his physical body. For thirty-eight years he paid the price of his consequences.

Sin can cause the greatest of men to suffer, but what gets my attention in this passage is this man's persistence to keep coming. Every day he came to the water's edge to get his miracle, and for thirty-eight years he went home in the same condition as when he came. Then the question comes: "Wilt thou be made whole?" The man answered, "I have no one to put me in…"

FAVOR KEY #6: FAVOR ISN'T DEPENDENT UPON ANYONE'S ACTIONS BUT YOUR OWN.

I have no one to put me in. And while I am coming to get the miracle someone steps over me.
—JOHN 5:7, AUTHOR'S PARAPHRASE

Have you ever been hurt by someone? When you needed a friend or a family member the most, they just seemed to be disinterested in what you needed. When you left their presence you felt hollow and hurt, feeling as though they stepped over you or on top of you. If you allow these kinds of situations to affect you, they will cause you to become bitter and angry. You will begin to build a wall around you that keeps others out. Oh, at first you will try to act like they didn't even bother you, but as time proceeds, the enemy will just keep pouring salt in the wound of pain and hurt until Satan drives you into a cave. A cave of loneliness, a cave of despair, a cave of depression and a cave of defeat will become your only counselors.

This kind of attack usually drives you neither to God nor His people, but away from God and those who could help you out of your problem.

Life has a way of defeating your faith. This is the reason that persistence is the fragrance that will attract God's favor. What we lack in the body of Christ is the power to stay put until God shows up with our miracle.

Pain and hurt are a part of the process of life. Get used to it! Every day isn't going to be grandiose. Hang onto your faith...faith has the ability to hold in times of trouble long enough for God to show up.

This one man came 13,870 times. He kept coming while others through the years quit. He just didn't sit around in his self-pity and have a pity party about his condition. He kept coming daily, believing and hoping that that would be the day he would be able to get in and walk home well.

Pity parties are the loneliest parties you will ever attend. *The only one at the party will be you!*

For thirty-eight years this man had been trying to get into the water of healing, when all of a sudden favor showed up in his life. The water came to him...healing water...sweet water...living water. This man was made whole by his persistence to keep on when others would have quit years ago.

Right now you may feel like quitting. DON'T! Don't quit that church! Don't quit giving! Don't quit praising and worshiping. You could be twenty-four hours from your fragrance to attracting God's favor. The miracle may be scheduled for tomorrow; don't quit today. Hang on; believe God that it's coming.

However long it is taking your harvest to manifest is a clue to how big your harvest is. Nothing big comes overnight. A big miracle takes time to set up and arrange.

Keep the faith! You're about to experience favor, and when it hits, it will make no sense.

CHAPTER 5

PROSPERITY, THE FRUIT OF FAVOR

The prosperity message has taken a lot of attack. One of the reasons I believe there has been a mass attack on prosperity is the misrepresentation we have encountered through the years. Ministers and people alike can mess up what was supposed to be a message to "set up and bless up."

The prosperity message isn't about money, yet money is a part of the prosperity message. Prosperity is much more than money. The Bible speaks about prosperity; it uses the word with multiple meanings. These meanings are well-being, happiness, healthiness, financial freedom and wholeness.

How can anyone attack a message that claims to promote wholeness? Anyone who puts down sowing and reaping has a hint from Satan in their words. Only the spirit of hell would put down a message that frees people to fulfill their destiny.

The Word of God is clear on prosperity:

> Sing unto the LORD, O ye saints of his, and give thanks at the remembrance of his holiness. For his anger endureth but a moment; in his favour is life: weeping may endure for a night, but joy cometh in

23

the morning. And in my prosperity I said, I shall
never be moved. LORD, by thy favour thou hast made
my mountain to stand strong: thou didst hide thy
face, and I was troubled.

—PSALM 30:4–7, KJV

Let them shout for joy, and be glad, that favour my
righteous cause: yea, let them say continually, Let the
LORD be magnified, which hath pleasure in the prosperity of his servant. And my tongue shall speak of
thy righteousness and of thy praise all the day long.

—PSALM 35:27–28, KJV

This one is one of my favorites. "Shout for joy." Why?
The Lord takes pleasure in my prosperity. The Lord loves
to see His children walking under the umbrella of His
blessing. Giving blessings to His children is what makes
the Lord happy.

To walk in prosperity you must have first fulfilled the
requirement to receive prosperity, which is the fruit of
favor.

Save now, I beseech thee, O LORD: O LORD, I
beseech thee, send now prosperity. Blessed be he that
cometh in the name of the LORD: we have blessed
you out of the house of the LORD

—PSALM 118:25–26, KJV

Pray for the peace of Jerusalem: they shall prosper that
love thee. Peace be within thy walls, and prosperity
within thy palaces. For my brethren and companions'
sakes, I will now say, Peace be within thee. Because of
the house of the LORD our God I will seek thy good.

—PSALM 122:6–9, KJV

In the day of prosperity be joyful…

—ECCLESIASTES 7:14, KJV

Cry yet, saying, thus saith the LORD of hosts; My cities through prosperity shall yet be spread abroad; and the LORD shall yet comfort Zion, and shall yet choose Jerusalem.

—ZECHARIAH 1:17, KJV

If they obey and serve him, they shall spend their days in prosperity, and their years in pleasures. But if they obey not, they shall perish by the sword, and they shall die without knowledge.

—JOB 36:11–12, KJV

Aren't these passages awesome? They carry such power and influence. The enemy doesn't want us to have anything to do with these passages. If they ever sink in, they will change your perspective and in return mess up the enemy. Read them again, remember them, and quote them. They will liberate you from lack and poverty.

How much favor can we expect from the Lord? Whatever it takes for God to fulfill what He has purposed for you. You should live no less for God than you lived for the enemy. However low you sank ought to be at least how high you rise. If you want to build a skyscraper, you first have to dig deep into the earth and build a proper foundation. The sign of your greatness is in the struggle it took to get here.

ARE THERE LEVELS OF FAVOR?

I have been asked if there are levels of favor. I thought for some time and found the answer in the Word of God. The answer to the question is *yes*. Indeed, there are levels of favor!

Let thy mercy, O LORD, be upon us, according as we hope in thee.

—PSALM 33:22, KJV

Mercy is none other than favor. "Let thy favor, O Lord, be upon us, according as we hope in thee." Favor is given at the level of hope. Hope is the substance of faith. So your faith level determines your favor level. Isn't that awesome? You can determine what level of favor you desire to walk in by walking in faith.

Great faith produces great favor. That's the reason you don't have everything you need sitting in your hand. God wants you to trust Him for your increase. He wants to be the ingredient that got you out. Prosperity is the fruit of favor.

The Lord will never allow you to do it completely alone. He will always keep something in your atmosphere that, without Him, you will never succeed.

When Moses was getting ready to become the deliverer of God's people, the Lord said something that I believe applies to what I'm writing about:

> And I am sure that the king of Egypt will not let you go, no, not by a mighty hand.
>
> —EXODUS 3:19, KJV

God right there clarifies how this whole thing of favor works. The enemy, which is in this case the king of Egypt, will not let you go; no, not by a mighty hand.

You're not going to make this happen by your mighty hand.

FAVOR KEY #7: ABILITIES ALONE WILL NOT PRODUCE FAVOR

If you could make it happen, it wouldn't be favor. Favor is when something greater has to join up with you and produce your provision to get you out of every circumstance that's been holding you down.

God says go and preach deliverance, but know this, Moses, Pharaoh is not going to budge, not by thy mighty hand.

> And I will stretch out my hand, and smite Egypt with all my wonders which I will do in the midst thereof: and after that he will let you go. And I will give this people favour in the sight of the Egyptians: and it shall come to pass, that, when ye go, ye shall not go empty.
>
> —EXODUS 3:20–21, KJV

God said, "But I will show these people favor. When I begin to show them favor, what you couldn't do with your might, I will do with favor." *What we can't get done in the natural, God will do with favor (the supernatural).* We have to just hold on even though we may have felt the struggle is in vain. God is about to show us favor, and our promotion is on the way. When we come out, we will not come out *empty-handed.*

These slaves came out full of God's provision. They were bent over with the blessing of favor. One day they were stomping around mud and making bricks for their taskmasters. The next day they were stomping around their enemy's homes, picking up the silk, pointing out the goods for the journey. Even with all of their abilities, the Israelites could not have made the Egyptians voluntarily give up their precious possessions.

Prosperity is the fruit of favor.

The children of Israel never had to plunder again while they were in the wilderness. God had provided enough for the journey. Favor always supplies the goods for the vision that God is in. *Provision for the vision.*

Favor is not money, yet favor can get you money! Favor always produces financial harvest. Money is one of the most misunderstood commodities in the church arena. Money has been looked at by fundamentalists as evil and wrong, and if you have it, you did something wrong to get it. When I say prosperity, you may want me to leave money out of the equation; however, money is the biggest portion of the equation.

Let me ask a question: If money is so evil, why do we keep it when we get it? Something that evil should be expelled immediately! Why is it so hard to get people to give it to further the kingdom of God? Wouldn't it make more sense to take evil money and turn it over to God and His work? I know that these questions sound silly, but so does the religious church when it tries to convince people that God isn't concerned about money. The truth is that God is very concerned about our prosperity and therefore about money.

The gospel has the power to deliver! The gospel has the power to set people free! The gospel when proclaimed can bring the meanest, angriest person to his knees. Only in the proclamation of the gospel of Jesus Christ can a whole congregation be touched at their level and at their need.

Recently I was sitting in a church service at The River Church in Raleigh, North Carolina. While Pastor Sheryl Brady began to develop her message and preach, I was moved at my place of need, and others were moved at theirs. Here's the power of the gospel.

Now what good is it if we have the power to set people free but can't go or do anything with that power? Nothing!

Money is the power of movement. Money is an amplifier!

Whatever it attaches itself to, it will amplify. If you're a drug addict and money is placed in your hands, you become a better drug addict. Money doesn't set you free. Money is not made to set you free. Money was made to lighten the load and give the power of movement to whatever it attaches itself. Now Satan has mastered this power, and the world gets richer while the church becomes poorer. When money is put into good ministry, it gives that ministry the power of movement. It doesn't just affect those in the local congregation, but it also begins to grow exponentially! Money attached to a business gives it the power to grow. The company now has the freedom to buy advertisements, build better offices, buy better equipment and hire better employees. Money is the power of movement!

We call money currency. Currency means a continual passing from hand to hand as a medium of exchange to get the job done.

Does that sound evil? Of course not! We have made it evil because we don't want to take the time to learn how to use money. The truth is that money is a current. It has the ability to cause flow and momentum. When used properly, money becomes a powerful resource. Money is not to sit still in someone's mattress so they can have it for a later date. It's not made to sit in your pocket to collect lint!

Money was created for increase. When money is placed in its proper environment, it reproduces at an incredible rate. Look what the world can do with money. Take a look around you. Look at the nightclubs, hotels and amusement parks. Watch the television channels such as Nickelodeon, MTV, VH1 and so many others. Millions of dollars are spent each year just to reach our children, yet in the local church we can't even raise $30,000 to send our youth to camp. We wonder why the world seems to be gaining converts while the church is losing them.

This isn't a book on money, but for me to take us to the next point, I need to build a bridge.

Prosperity is the fruit of favor.

If money is a power source for movement, why doesn't the church have more of it? Great question.

The number one reason is that we can't handle what money does when we get it. If you can't tithe on a $50,000 annual income, do you think you would tithe on a million? The truth is, the more money you obtain, the harder it is to give it. It's one thing to give a ten-dollar bill or a one hundred dollar bill, but let that surge to multiple thousands. You start rationalizing in your mind, *This is entirely too much money for us to give to our church.* You begin to rewrite your theology; therefore, God doesn't allow too much money to cross your path. By keeping you small, He keeps you faithful.

When the Lord can trust you with little, He will most certainly overwhelm you with much.

CHAPTER 6

ACTIONS THAT STOP THE FLOW OF FAVOR

There are six actions that will stop favor from flowing in your life.

I. IGNORANCE

Ignorance will stop the flow of favor. It's not what you know that's killing you; it's what you don't know.

Ignorance doesn't mean you're stupid or unable to learn. Ignorance is the lack of knowledge. I believe that ignorance is when people decide not to listen and not to change—staying stuck in your traditions even when you know that times are changing. Tradition is a look of the past. A vision is a look of the future.

Ignorance is when you don't want to learn. You just stay stuck in the middle of your mind-set, and you never let anyone or anything teach or train you to change.

We need to immediately start making movement away from people who are unwilling to learn or change. Anyone who is not willing to change will try to stop your desire for change.

Change isn't progress in life; change is the price we pay

31

for progress. Ignorance stops the power of change. Ignorance also stops the power of synergy and flow. If your company is going to grow, if your church is going to grow, if your home is going to grow...it is going to require two things. Synergy and flow!

Synergy is the ability to get in step with others, and flow is the by-product of synergy. When a dance team wants to win in a dance contest, they begin to practice long hours. They are developing synergy, the ability to sync together and feel each other's moves. When this happens, they have flow.

Synergy is a combined effort. Combined effort! Nothing is going to grow large without the work and efforts of the whole crew. Synergy is the combined efforts of the team. When synergy begins to sync up your staff and then your leaders, they begin to combine their efforts for the flow of one vision, your corporation or church.

Flow is the power of movement in the same direction. When water begins to flow in the same direction, it begins to take on dangerous force and power. Sometimes the History Channel or Weather Channel will broadcast shows on water or floods. The power of water is amazing. When the force of water beats on something continuously, it begins to weaken its structure until the water overpowers whatever it has been beating on. The same is true with any corporation or organization. When we synchronize with others, we become a unit. *That means we are now in unity.*

> How good and pleasant it is when brothers live together in unity! It is like precious oil poured on the head, running down on the beard, running down on Aaron's beard, down upon the collar of his robes. It is as if the dew of Hermon were falling on Mount

Zion. For there the LORD bestows his blessing, even
life forevermore.

—PSALM 133:1–3

Ignorance can stop the power of synergy and flow. You
need to stop anyone from coming into your access who is
unwilling to learn or change. They are not your friend;
they are your enemy. My mentor, Dr. Mike Murdock, says
your enemy is anyone who weakens your focus and trivi-
alizes your passion. Ignorance will weaken your focus and
murder your passion.

2. DISOBEDIENCE

Disobedience is a crippling act to the children of God.
The Lord will never allow you to walk in big blessings if
He can't trust you with little acts of obedience.

When we disobey the Lord, we are telling Him that we
don't reverence Him or respect Him. When I was a child,
my father would leave me instructions to cut the yard or
weed out the flowerbed. The first thing I would do when
I got home from school or woke up on a Saturday morning was obey him. I would immediately cut the grass or
do whatever he had instructed me to do when he left for
work that morning. Now, let's get something straight. It's
not that I got up or came home excited about doing what
I was instructed to do. Not at all! I did it because I kept a
mental and physical picture of the consequences of the
last time I disobeyed his instructions. His pain on my
backside caused me to obey the next time.

My father was one of those fathers from the old school.
He wasn't going to let you do anything or go anywhere
until you had carried out his instructions. However, when
I was obedient to his instructions, there would be a
reward. When it came time for me to do something with

my friends or to take a date out on Friday night, he would hand me money or the keys to his car without hesitation. My obedience caused favor to flow from his hand to mine. Sometimes he would ask if I had money, and he would slip me more if I only had a little. I would shout all the way to wherever I was going. Favor is much better than correction. I experienced less pain and more blessings because I learned the power of obedience.

Doesn't this sound a lot like the Word of God? When we walk in obedience, we walk in God's favor. Disobedience stops the flow of favor.

FAVOR KEY #8: GOD WILL NOT TAKE YOU PAST YOUR LAST ACT OF DISOBEDIENCE.

We will never advance to the next level unless we are willing to be obedient.

Job 36:11 says that if we serve and obey God, we will live our days in prosperity and our years in pleasure.

Isaiah 1:19 says that if you are willing and obedient, you shall eat the good of the land.

Obedience is the key to God's favor. The Lord knows that He can trust you when He sees your acts of obedience. When God was ready to take Abraham to the next level, the Word of God says that God tested or tempted Abraham— God asked Abraham to offer his only son Isaac.

This was the test of obedience. God will always qualify those He is about to promote. Let me give you the first step to greatness based on Genesis 22:1–14; it is *submission first.*

Abraham first had to be submissive to the plans and commands of the Lord. *When agreement ends, submission begins.* There can be no submission until you have received instructions with which you don't agree, but you follow anyway. I can't imagine Abraham being in agreement with God on the instructions to kill his only son, can you? I can see submission! We won't always agree with the instructions of the Lord, but we must always submit. Submission is the power of obedience. When we obey, we open up the windows of heaven. But when we disobey, we stop the flow of God's favor.

Submission is often viewed as a weakness. The truth is that most great leaders who are in leadership started out being submissive. They were either helping others to gain their greatness or learning from people who were ahead of them.

It takes a great sense of security to be a servant. When we are walking in agreement, both parties are responsible for the cost and outcome of their journey. When they come to the crossroads of disagreement, the servant must take on the role of submission. They will disqualify themselves for the consequences of the decision and qualify for the harvest when they do.

Let me explain. To be in agreement, you must be willing to follow. You must be willing to submit to the one who is with you even if you do not exactly agree with the decision. If that decision was the right decision for the corporation or church to take, then the one who submitted is also entitled to the spoils of the journey. If the decision was wrong, then the leader will bear the brunt of the mistake alone. Thus, the servant qualifies for the spoils and has disqualified for the judgment of the mistake. That is awesome!

If we could only understand this principle, we could slow down the exoduses in most organizations. For most people believe that agreement is submission. Not so! When a people or families in our churches disagree with the bishop or pastor, they immediately leave, assuming that they have been in submission all the time. Yet that's not true. They have actually been in agreement with the leader, not in submission. *Submission can only begin when agreement ends.*

On Mother's Day my wife, Pastor Maryann, preached on the power of a woman, and in her message she spoke powerfully and eloquently on submission. She made a statement that was liberating. "When we choose to walk in submission to the Word of God, God allows us the power to travail through and receive our harvest or promise. The key to victory is being able to prevail long enough that you outlast the storms."

3. Covetousness

To covet is when you desire what another person has, and in the process of wanting what others have you are never satisfied with what you have.

This can be very stressful for those who are always living their lives evaluating what others have. We begin to compare ourselves with others when we covet. The problem with this is that we will always come up with the short end of the stick.

We will always compare their strengths to our weaknesses when we compare ourselves with others. So in the equation we will always come up wanting what others have. Coveting can destroy churches; coveting can destroy friendships.

> You shall not covet your neighbor's house. You shall not covet your neighbor's wife, or his manservant or maidservant, his ox or donkey, or anything that belongs to your neighbor.
>
> —Exodus 20:17

> You shall not covet your neighbor's wife. You shall
> not set your desire on your neighbor's house or land,
> his manservant or maidservant, his ox or donkey, or
> anything that belongs to your neighbor.
>
> —DEUTERONOMY 5:21

To covet is to delight yourself in the goods and wealth of others. People are usually having identity deprivation when they covet what their neighbor has. They lack confidence in themselves and usually estimate their self-worth by what they own, drive or live in. The problem with this curse is that you will never have enough. When you think you have accomplished your desired goal, your neighbor will drive up in a new car, or your friend will buy a bigger house, and then you're right back in the circle of dissatisfaction.

The key side effect of covetousness is frustration! You will continue to live a life of frustration if you measure your self-worth with materialism instead of what God says about you in His Word. Frustration will cause you to make wrong decisions, and wrong decisions will result in depletion.

Covetousness will stop the flow of favor.

4. GREED

Greed is when you can't let go of what you have. Greed is the opposite of coveting; yet, I like to say that greed and covetousness are brothers. They walk hand in hand. You have proven that what you own owns you if you are not willing to let go of it! *Greed* is defined by Webster's dictionary as "excessive desire for getting or having, esp. wealth; desire for more than one needs or deserves."

The proof of greed is shown every week in most church services. You are walking in the spirit of greed if you feel angry or lose your joy when the offering is received.

Think for just one moment. What do you have that God didn't let you have anyway? Nothing. So when it comes time to put back into the kingdom of God, you would think that people would be joyous to help the church grow.

I can't think of a better way to cure the curse of greed than through giving. Giving is a sure sign that you have conquered the spirit of greed. Giving is a sure sign that you possess the Spirit of the Lord. After all, God is a giver! He gave His best seed, Jesus. Should He expect anything less from you?

Greed will always stop the flow of favor. Greed will stop the flow of money very fast. Greed is selfishness personified.

5. PRIDE

Then there's pride. Pride is when you love yourself so much that no one can even get close enough to help you. When people walk in pride, they lack the ability to be taught.

Have you ever run into someone who, no matter what you talked about, always knew more? When you hang around these kinds of people, it doesn't take long to build up a dislike for them. Their pride is causing you to run. Pride comes before destruction.

Pride is also a part of a nongiver's life. When you're not a giver, you are saying that you don't need anyone, that you don't care about anyone and that you don't need God. Pride makes us an island unto ourselves. Now, I don't know about you, but I do not want to be left to myself for very long. I will do more damage to myself than my enemy would. People who walk in pride are usually a legend in their own minds.

6. ANGER AND BITTERNESS

Last are anger and bitterness. Bitterness is the result of walking in anger for so long that you have lost the ability to forgive others.

Anger is a wall that blocks others out. Anger left alone can destroy you. When you are hurt by others, or by life, you need to develop the attitude that, no matter what, God will take care of the situation. Don't let the sun go down on your anger. If you go to bed with that offense in place, you will be giving that anger time to birth a seed in your spirit. That seed when it comes to maturity is bitterness. Notice the difference between the words *bitter* and *better*—there's only one letter that separates them. That letter is the letter *I*. That's right. In my life the only way to survive is for me to make up my mind not to allow the offense to take root. I am the deciding factor between bitter or better.

What about you? Has someone hurt you so badly that you hurt over your wound? Have you been a person who has been carrying a load of anger? Maybe you're a woman whose husband has left you holding all the responsibilities or left you with a house full of children and a load of bills. Are you carrying a load of anger with regard to your past or what your father or mother did or didn't do? Or are you someone who just doesn't know how to deal with those who talk directly to you? There are many ways we can be wounded.

The truth is, life will always cut us, and people will always disappoint us. Remember this: Wounded people leak issues. Hurting people hurt people! Healthy people heal people.

Anger, if not dealt with, will kill any chance for God to bless you. Anger has a way of tearing down every good thing about you. Anger is a doorway to other problems— problems such as *bitterness, lack of trust, fear, worry, perception problems, strife, gossip, pride, insecurity, inability to love others, loneliness* and so many others.

Right now, if you have been hit by any or all of these symptoms, then quickly...don't delay...repent...so that favor will start flowing to your life.

Pray this prayer right now:

> *Lord, I'm sorry. I've been hurt. Forgive me for allowing the hurts of my life to block Your flow of favor. Lord, forgive me for my pride, forgive me for my ignorance, and forgive me for my disobedience. Lord, forgive me for my greed and covetousness.*
>
> *Lord, I need Your guidance. I need Your understanding. Teach me Your ways.*
>
> *Help me to walk according to the law of favor. I speak right now that all my hurts and messes are over today. I will not carry them one more day, for today I have been set free from the wounds of my past. I will not walk in condemnation over what I am unable to go back and fix. However, I will look forward to my life of favor.*
>
> *I am highly favored of the Lord today!*
> *Amen!*

CHAPTER 7

FAVOR WILL TAKE YOU ANYWHERE BUT BACKWARDS

Let me paint a picture on how I see the story of Elijah and Elisha that is found in 1 Kings 19.

> So Elijah went from there and found Elisha son of Shaphat. He was plowing with twelve yoke of oxen, and he himself was driving the twelfth pair. Elijah went up to him and threw his cloak around him. Elisha then left his oxen and ran after Elijah. "Let me kiss my father and mother good-by," he said, "and then I will come with you."
> "Go back," Elijah replied. "What have I done to you?"
> —1 Kings 19:19–20

It was a hot day. The air was cloudy, and it was hard to breathe from the dust of the freshly plowed fields. The young man behind the ox was tired for he had worked all day to reach his deadline to have the fields ready for seed.

Sowing time was rapidly approaching, and Elisha was putting in long hard days to meet his deadline. It was Elisha's profession to plow up the fields on time. Elisha was the owner of the plowing association. He had twelve plows and twelve oxen. He was not only the owner, but he was also one of the workers. He himself plowed with the eleven other workers.

Elisha, who had reached success at a young age, seemed to have lost his passion for the corporation that he had built by himself. He was walking behind his ox, as he had done so many days before, but this day was different. He seemed to drift off into a daydream more than once trying to keep his furrows straight. He was wondering why he was so unfulfilled. He was full of potential to do and be something else, but he was stuck. Stuck right here behind an ox trying to make sense of his life. Elisha was stuck in the rut of life, and he knew he ought to be grateful and full of joy. After all, no one in his village had accomplished so much in such a short time.

He looked back at his workers who were jovial, laughing and enjoying their success with their owner Elisha. "What is wrong with me?" he cried out with tears flowing down his dirt-smeared cheeks, dripping onto the dried field and making mud in the rut of life.

Elisha had a question that was haunting him: "What am I to do with the rest of my life? Is this it? Will I stay here and never see the world beyond the butt of this ox?"

I know what some are thinking, and for many years I thought the same way. Elisha should be grateful and thankful that he had accomplished so much as a young man. I tend to disagree with that concept today. Elisha had a vocation, but inside he had been selected and possessed the power of potential. He was feeling the tug of the spirit that whispered, "There's more...there's more to your life than an ox and a plow."

I call this the question of potential. God will never allow satisfaction to come into someone's life when there is a potential for greatness locked up inside of them no matter how much money they make, how big their house is or how many cars they own. They have the potential to do something besides build houses, drive cars and earn money. Every time they walk into the yard, they have this lonely sense...this gnawing feeling that there is something else they ought to be doing. They cry out, "What's wrong with me?" If you are like they are, no one will understand you— not your family, not your friends, not your spouse, not your coworkers. As a matter of fact, they'll all think you're crazy. Most likely you'll think you're going crazy, too.

Look at Elisha's situation, plowing behind an ox. The ox is a strong animal. It can pull great weight and do it with great ease. Strong, but dumb! Elisha had been plowing behind that dumb thing long enough. Aren't you tired of the dumb things and the dumb decisions that have weighed you down with problems and heartache? The world is full of people who live a life that they hate, wishing they could start over and make the right decisions where they made the wrong ones. Unfortunately, you can't go back and fix what you have already messed up. However, you can look back and learn. Learn what dumb thing you did that caused the consequences of your present. You can use the power of reflection to learn how to achieve greatness in your future.

The truth of the matter is that every one of us has made dumb and stupid decisions that have cost us greatly. We have all looked at our lives at one time and wondered what in the world went wrong. Those who can do this and fight the spirit of depression and failure will climb out of their pit and accomplish in their future what they were unable to conquer in their past. When you find your place in life unfulfilling, and you can't seem to get a grip on your emotions, you might be hearing the inner voice of the Spirit whispering, "There's more...there's more to your life than an ox and a plow." You might be feeling the tugging of a greater potential. You may be feeling the seed of your baby of destiny cresting at the end of the womb of your future.

Then there's the plow... digging up the dirt of a field day after day. Elisha's life had become mundane. Imagine a life of doing the same thing over and over again and having to deal with rocks, stones and roots, or engaging a fight with the hard soil of life and having to do it with no passion. This could have been the place where Elisha would begin to weaken his spiritual walk if he didn't deal with his frustrations soon.

Elisha was fed up with the lifestyle of his present. Not that his lifestyle was wrong or bad; it was just that this young man had a destiny, and that destiny was about to come knocking on the door of his life. God was preparing him for the entrance of a father. Here Elisha is asking a question, and he has no answer. A question with no answer can be frustrating.

Let's leave Elisha for a moment and journey across the desert to Beersheba in Judah.

Elijah was sitting in a dry place in life, depressed, tired and wishing he was dead. Imagine this, a major prophet anointed by God... a man of God who had not just performed one major miracle, but several, and at his last miracle he called down fire on Mount Carmel and ended a three-year drought that he himself had prophesied. This miracle was the catalyst of all his miracles. He had faced the prophets of Baal in one of the greatest face-offs in the Bible.

> Elijah went before the people and said, "How long will you waver between two opinions? If the LORD is God, follow him; but if Baal is God, follow him." But the people said nothing.

Then Elijah said to them, "I am the only one of the LORD's prophets left, but Baal has four hundred and fifty prophets. Get two bulls for us. Let them choose one for themselves, and let them cut it into pieces and put it on the wood but not set fire to it. I will prepare the other bull and put it on the wood but not set fire to it. Then you call on the name of your god, and I will call on the name of the LORD. The god who answers by fire—he is God."

—1 KINGS 18:21–24

Elijah faced these four hundred and fifty prophets of Baal all by himself, and when it was over, he had called down fire from heaven. Elijah's God was the God who had answered. The end result, Elijah ordered all the prophets of Baal to be slaughtered.

Now here was this major prophet running from a queen named Jezebel...all because she sent him a threat that she would do to him what he did to her prophets. This is crazy. He had the faith to believe for fire on a watered-down altar, but he lacked the faith to face Jezebel.

Elijah was afraid and ran for his life. When he came to Beersheba in Judah, he left his servant there, while he himself went a day's journey into the desert. He came to a broom tree, sat down under it and prayed that he might die. "I have had enough, LORD," he said. "Take my life; I am no better than my ancestors." Then he lay down under the tree and fell asleep.

—1 KINGS 19:3–5

This was no ordinary prophet. He was the chief of all the prophets who led the school of the prophets. What happened to him? This old prophet was sick of his life and sick of fighting the king and queen of the land. He was tired of taking three steps forward and two steps backwards. The story continues:

> All at once an angel touched him and said, "Get up and eat." He looked around, and there by his head was a cake of bread baked over hot coals, and a jar of water. He ate and drank and then lay down again.
>
> The angel of the LORD came back a second time and touched him and said, "Get up and eat, for the journey is too much for you." So he got up and ate and drank. Strengthened by that food, he traveled forty days and forty nights until he reached Horeb, the mountain of God. There he went into a cave and spent the night.
>
> —1 KINGS 19:3–9

How did Elijah get into this dark and wet place in life? After all, Jezebel had only threatened him; she had never laid a hand on this man of God. Sometimes words can do more damage than being physically attacked. Physical wounds heal in weeks. Verbal wounds, if received, take years, and sometimes a lifetime, to heal. When we receive verbal threats, we tend to internalize those words to untruths. Elijah was in a cave because he let his enemy come into his mind and thus perceived her threat as truth, when in actuality it was a lie. The truth: Jezebel was never going to get close enough to attack this man of God. God had plans for Elijah, and those plans were to father a spiritual son.

Life has a way of driving you into the cave of despair and depression. Never let anyone or anything cause you to flee into the cave of isolation. All you will ever end up with in a cave is tunnel vision. In the cave you can only focus on what you are going through and not what you can go to. Satan loves to put us into the cave of fear...the cave of regret...the cave of lack and doubt. You will never do anything while you remain in the isolation of the cave.

Elijah became so focused on his problem that he began to lose focus of his destination. How about you? Have you become so consumed with your present circumstance or situation that you have begun to lose your focus on the total plan for your life? Has desperation already set in?

God may anoint us for ministry, but isn't it interesting that He anoints us alongside our weaknesses? God allows these weaknesses to stay intact so that we won't become so lost in our own works that we forget for whom we are doing them.

God appeared to Elijah in his hideout and began to paint a picture beyond his present situation. He showed him his future, and God spoke to Elijah and told him, "Go; you have a son to birth and mentor. Your predecessor is waiting for you!" Now Elijah had the answer but no question, but the question was waiting for the answer to cross his path.

Elijah needed to take another look. He needed to look beyond his storm...beyond his present situation and focus on his future. If God has spoken a word over you, don't panic.

God showed up, and Elijah came out of the cave. God gave him instructions to anoint two kings—one of which would deal with Jezebel—and anoint a predecessor to carry on his mantle when he was taken up to heaven. That predecessor was Elisha. Elisha had a question, Elijah had the answer, and the two were about to cross paths. It's at this crossroads in life that greatness is forged. Here is where we find transfers taking place. The Pauls transform the Timothys...the Naomis transform the Ruths...the Jonathans transform the Davids. It's at this place in life we must recognize whom God has sent across our path to change our focus and move us from ordinary to extraordinary—when the answer has finally found your question.

Imagine what Elisha must have thought when he saw Elijah walking across his freshly plowed field. It must have unnerved him greatly. "What is this old man doing walking across my freshly plowed field? Does he have any idea how much time and effort it has taken me to finish this task? And here he comes stomping and messing up all the work I have done! Messing up what I have spent a lifetime trying to clean up. Stirring up what I thought was hidden. Moving things around that cause me to see what I really don't desire to see. I'm stuck in this rut...am I willing to let someone challenge me to change?"

The first step to change is allowing God to walk right on top of your life's work and dreams, and let Him step into your present to create your future. When the call of destiny has entered your present to ignite you for your future, it will not come in the way that you would most likely want it to. If you don't recognize that, even though it came in and messed up your picture-perfect day, you will stay stuck in the rut of life! Let destiny walk right on top of your freshly plowed life. For when you are finished, you will never regret that you did!

When Elisha turned to the man of God, he asked him to let him go home and tell his mother and father good-bye. Elijah said, "Go home or go back, for what have I done to you?"

It's what Elisha did that is so powerful. He walked over to his plow and ox and began to chop up his plow and slaughter his ox. Imagine Elijah watching and wondering what in the world had gotten into this young man. I'll tell you! He wanted to burn his bridge of temptation. He wanted to let you and me know that when the journey gets hard, or when those times come when he would be frustrated and angry at his spiritual father and was tempted to quit or go home, he couldn't. Elisha knew that favor would take you anywhere but backwards.

Following the call of God should never be easy. Questions arise in my heart about the sincerity of the call, especially when people with hardly any training come to me and say that they are called into the ministry. When you try to use them in areas that are of servant value, they complain. They say things like, "I'm anointed to preach... I'm called to the platform...God has bigger things for me." The truth is, if you're not willing to do the small things, then you will never get to do the large things.

FAVOR KEY #9: IF YOU CAN'T BE CORRECTED, YOU CAN'T BE CONNECTED.

For us to walk in favor, we must be willing to sit under the feet of a spiritual father. One great spiritual father to me is Bishop Joby Brady. He is the type of man of God that when he sees things that are out of place or wrong for your ministry, he tells you. When you encounter these prophets, let them walk all over your freshly plowed fields because they have entered your life to change it. You will make for yourself a God connection when you do. Correction is connection!

Favor is so much more than money or materialism. Favor is the power of access. It is the ability to get in someone's presence who can add to your life in such a way that they will cause you to go to the next level faster than if you try to go alone. No great man ever did anything great alone. People need people to grow. Men need fathers for identity, for instructions and for impartation.

Favor is the result of your serving someone favored.

When you serve someone, you will win their favor, and they will eventually give *you* what *they* have—*favor!*

Access is more powerful than money. When the right men notice you, they will help promote you. Favor comes when the Lord starts to put His seal of approval on you. Then others notice something about you that causes them to want to help you. When favor is on you, you will find yourself in places and around people where you do not belong, and you know that favor put you there. Favor will get you promoted faster; favor will call you away from your mundane lifestyle and have you following your greatness.

Elisha had a question, and favor was bringing him the answer. Let me mentor you in favor: Just because God sends the right man to help and guide you doesn't mean that you are going to be able to make this decision with ease.

I'm sure it was hard for Elisha to walk away from his security blanket. Anytime we follow the call of God, it always starts out hard. Faith is built when we survive bad situations and hard places. Favor and faith are cousins; for you to walk in the F.O.G. (the favor of God), you are going to have to be able to step out into the land of unfamiliarity. You will have to be willing to walk out into the sea of darkness with nothing more to lean on but the voice of the Lord saying, "Come." If Peter hadn't been willing to step over the side of that boat in Matthew 14, he would have never accomplished the supernatural and walked on water. When you are stepping in the storm-raging sea of life and unfamiliarity, you know you're going to be okay if favor has stepped out with you. Favor won't go where the Word of God hasn't sent you or isn't calling you. Favor will not take you where the Lord is not sending you.

Elisha's next level of life wasn't going to be easy. Faith

is never easy. Faith requires you to step out on nothing but the Word of God. Faith is when you believe the God you serve enough to walk away from everything, solely relying on the spoken word of God. It's at this level that we see men being born to greatness. Those who are willing to trust God, and walk and serve until God promotes them, will always accomplish great things!

Elisha left the life of self-employment and entered into the life of God-employment. The mind of the unlearned and immature would immediately assume that entering into the employment of God is going to be easy and full of rewards. The truth is, rewards do come, but not until after testing and trial. God will only release what He can trust you with. The first step will be the life of a servant before you live the life of a king. Timing will become the student's greatest asset—timing to know when your time is and not to let your mind wander into the land of "I Can" and "I'm As Good As…"

Timing is the hinge on which the door of favor is hung, and faith is the key that unlocks that door. Giving is the power that forces the door of favor open, and when it does, your harvest will come…a big harvest! Favor is a seed before it is a harvest.

Favor Key #10: Whom You Are Connected With, You Will Eventually Become.

Elisha went from plowing his own way to plowing another man's way. He would spend the next fifteen years of his life pouring water on the hands of Elijah. During this process he was transformed and changed into another man, for the anointing that rested on Elijah one day would be poured into the life of Elisha. This is the transition stage of change; every day Elisha was willing to take

care of the man of God and pour water on his hands and
feet. In the eyes of others Elisha was just a servant, but in
the eyes of God he was ministering to the anointing that
he himself would one day carry. His physical pouring was
changing into a spiritual pouring.

Here's where ordinary men become great men. It's at
this level of servanthood and determination that you'll
see insignificant people becoming significant...ordinary
people becoming extraordinary. I'm sure there were times
when Elisha didn't agree with Elijah. I'm sure there were
rough times, hard days, sad moments and disturbing questions in the mind of Elisha, questions that we have all
asked at one time or another, like: "Have I done the right
thing?" "When will I get to do my ministry?" "Why is it
taking so long?" However, Elisha buried those feelings and
stayed clothed in the garment of being a good protégé.

There are two kinds of people connecting themselves
to you—parasites or protégés! There are those who are
adding to your life or those who are sucking the very life
from you. How can you tell who they are? Simple: If you
can't correct them, you don't connect them.

- A protégé wants to learn from you; a parasite
  wants to take from you.

- A protégé wants to gain your knowledge; a parasite wants to dispute your knowledge.

- A protégé is always thinking about the mentor's
  well-being; a parasite is always thinking about
  himself...he has the "what about me" syndrome.

- A protégé will offer to serve you no matter what;
  a parasite resents serving you.

- A protégé adds to your joy; a parasite takes from
  your joy.

Elisha was a good protégé. He knew when to speak and when to listen.

(Let me take a moment here to encourage you to read some of Dr. Mike Murdock's material on leadership.)

Elisha did what most people are unable to do...make the transition. He went from plowing to pouring. The key to your next season is the ability to take this journey of transition.

Success isn't necessarily the result of some great idea; success comes when we are able to make the transition from one season to the next.

Every season has a code of conduct. The capability to discover the code will determine the potential of your next season. When people do not discern this code, their present becomes permanent. Every member of the military is taught the proper code of conduct to the point that adherence to that code is required even if they're captured.

America is full of men and women who never go beyond their present situation and enter their next season. Why? They will not discover the code of conduct that is required of them.

The reasons are numerous. They may be afraid to make the leap of faith required. They may be afraid of the risk that is involved to make the crossing. They may be so clouded with anger and bitterness over their past and present that they cannot see their future potential. They may have been preconditioned by their parents, peers or associates that they would never amount to anything.

If you are determined to follow God's code of conduct for you in your next season, you will make the transition well and eventually become like the godly man or woman who was your father or mother in the faith.

FAVOR KEY #11: YOU WILL NEVER RISE ABOVE YOUR SELF-IMAGE.

Transition is the key to unlocking the code that has been encrypted all your life. The code to purpose is behind the door of transition. Elisha had the mental resources needed to make this transition. He proved that he possessed what was required to take his life to the next season when he destroyed the ox and the plow. The ability to burn bridges will cause you to stay focused on your future instead of on your past. You must decide in your heart that you will not look back for favor to take you anywhere. Favor will take you anywhere but backwards.

- Favor is not connected to your abilities.

- Favor is not hinged on the abilities to get the job done but the willingness to try.

- Favor is not looking for the gifted as much as it's looking for the willing.

- Favor is not looking for those who possess the power of understanding but those who have the readiness to obey understanding.

Our churches are full of those who understand truth but never operate in it. They just sit in the service week after week clocking time, and in their hearts they believe they are doing something great for God. The truth is, they haven't done anything for God in a long time.

Favor is not saying, "Well, if I have the abilities and the time, I'll do it." Favor doesn't sit by and wait to graduate from Harvard in order to be used. Favor will grab you as you do little things daily, turning them into great things. Favor will reach into the gutter of life and pull you out all because you were willing to burn your plow and cut up your oxen. Favor always looks for the underdog! Favor cheers for the insignificant and turns them into something great.

Favor will drag you, favor will pull you, and favor will drive you. Favor will take you anywhere but backwards.

Do yourself a favor and look as far as you can behind you. Look to your left...now look to your right...now look ahead of you, and *let that be the last time you ever look back.*

The Lord will never use you if you don't possess the power to chop up what's holding you back. *Deal with it!* You can never go forward until you are ready to deal with where you came from and make peace with your past so you can have power in your present and future. We all have things in our past that have hurt us, wounded us and almost destroyed us. Psalm 124:1 was written for all of us who have a past: "If the LORD had not been on our side," I would have died in my mess. Thank God I'm still here, and so are you. I have good news for you...your past has no bearing on where you are going. It doesn't matter what you've done in the past. God is willing and big enough to erase your mistakes. The problem with most of us is that we can't deal with our mistakes as efficiently as God deals with them. Satan loves to keep reminding us of all our bloopers and blunders.

God is not looking at our past. He's focused on our future, and it's time for the body of Christ to do the same. Favor will take us anywhere but backwards.

Elisha served Elijah for fifteen years. This would seem to be a long time for most twenty-first-century followers. Fifteen years! One of the greatest tests for promotion is the ability to wait on God. Waiting is the proof of trust. Timing is the power of accumulation. Learn to wait on things...in time we will eventually acquire our provisions.

> Even the youths shall faint and be weary, and the
> young men shall utterly fall: But they that wait upon
> the LORD shall renew their strength; they shall
> mount up with wings as eagles; they shall run, and
> not be weary; and they shall walk, and not faint.
>   —ISAIAH 40:30–31, KJV

When those in assistant leadership roles are not interested in self-promotion but are interested in the kingdom of God and its advancement, they will walk in a higher anointing than those who only care about when and where they are going to get promoted.

Let me give you the steps to Elisha's greatness:

1. The plowing
2. The pouring
3. The promotion
4. The performance
5. The prophecy

Here's where we as leaders must learn to grow. Between each step Elisha had to be able to make the transition. Transition is the key to greatness. Most people are unable to make the necessary adjustments so that they can go from one level to the next. Transition is uncomfortable. It is always hard to make, but it is the key to great favor.

Elisha accomplished in one day what it took Elijah a lifetime to accomplish because of transition. When we are faithful to go forward, make the necessary changes and walk with the right attitude through the valleys of transition, favor will take over—and favor will take us anywhere but backwards.

CHAPTER 8

†WO-MÎLE PERSOΠ ÎΠ A OΠE-MÎLE WORLD

C an you really pass the test? Is it possible to withstand whatever you're in...can you really hold up under a storm or hang on when calamity comes? *Absolutely!*

Some time later God tested Abraham. He said to him, "Abraham!"
"Here I am," he replied.
Then God said, "Take your son, your only son, Isaac, whom you love, and go to the region of Moriah. Sacrifice him there as a burnt offering on one of the mountains I will tell you about."
Early the next morning Abraham got up and saddled his donkey. He took with him two of his servants and his son Isaac. When he had cut enough wood for the burnt offering, he set out for the place God had told him about. On the third day Abraham looked up and saw the place in the distance. He said to his servants, "Stay here with the donkey while I and the boy go over there. We will worship and then we will come back to you."

—GENESIS 22:1–5

God tested Abraham to see what kind of worshiper he was, and God will test us also. God instructed Abraham to take his son Isaac across the desert to Mount Moriah. Here's a question for you: Why didn't God just ask Abraham to take his seed into the backyard and sacrifice him there? Real worship will always require something more from you than just a convenient stroll into the backyard. Real worship takes effort, concentration and focus. Real worship is unrehearsed.

That wasn't a day of joy or happiness. It was a day of pain and confusion. Don't think for one moment that Abraham knew what God was going to do. He had to walk in obedience that was a result of relationship. The one thing he had to depend on was his relationship with God. This wasn't going to be an easy task, not at all. Where did we come up with the theology that everything we do for God should be easy? We ought to do things for God that cause us to become uncomfortable. Abraham had one thing going for him; he understood what real worship required.

Real worship requires the attitude of pushing—pushing through your fears, pushing through your misunderstandings and pushing through your circumstances. Stay focused no matter what. When I was a youth pastor I would often use the acronym PUSH in my messages— Praise Until Something Happens!

Abraham was under the eyes of the teacher, and he had been handed the test. Abraham was subjected to act upon what he had been studying. He was called upon to go the second mile, to live above and beyond. In this trial, he would show what he was really made of. The pressures of life are sometimes the only way we can discover what we are really full of. What has been deposited will eventually come out under pressure.

Notice that Abraham told his servant "to stay here while the lad and I go over there. We will worship and then we will come back." Abraham wasn't told to go to worship—he was told to offer Isaac! You have to understand that when you are in the middle of trouble or a trial, when you have to face something that is wrecking you on the inside, there is one key ingredient that can turn the tide into your favor... *worship no matter what!*

FAVOR KEY #12: FAVOR IS THE BY-PRODUCT OF REAL WORSHIP.

Real worship can turn the tide of troubles in your favor.

Hezekiah was told by the prophet Elijah to get his house in order because he was going to die. Just because someone spoke a word over you doesn't necessarily mean that it is the final word.

Hezekiah turned his back to the wall and started worshiping God. Maybe his worship went something like this. "God, I don't want to die. Besides, Lord, no one can praise You like I praise You. Lord, the grave can't worship You like I worship You." His worship reached heaven and grabbed the heart of God; before the prophet could get out of the house, God had changed Hezekiah's outcome. What a story. Wouldn't you like to get an answer that quickly? Think about it; you just left the loan officer's office where you were turned down for a loan that you needed to get that new house, but before you could get out of the foyer of the bank the loan officer came running out after you and said, "Wait a minute; I've changed my mind." And *all because you left with the attitude of worship.*

Favor doesn't make any sense, nor does worship, especially when everything else around you is crying out for you to complain or whimper, but instead you throw your arms up and begin to worship. Suddenly, you hear the banker tell you he is not going to give you a loan for your new house...he is going to give you the house!

Real worship turns your circumstance from death or poverty into the revelation that you have a Jehovah-Jireh! You can only get that revelation if you are willing to offer an obedient sacrifice of worship in times of trouble, a sacrifice of praise, which is the fruit of your lips.

The test of greatness is in the ability to move beyond the line of mediocrity. The only way to move above being just average is to become a true worshiper.

With every step Abraham took up the mountain of worship, his provision was climbing up the other side at the same pace as his worship. Every anguished step up his mountain of uncertainty, every movement to push a little higher up his mountain of pain, the ram was on the other side moving toward the thicket. This is how God works. He first sets up the test; then through the test He teaches us His principles. When we pass the test, operating in His principles, we receive the promise or provision.

The pattern

The pattern is to push through, to keep going, to keep hanging on even though all hell has stacked itself against you. Faith isn't faith until it passes the test. Faith is confidence in God. When you doubt, you demonstrate that you have more faith in your adversity than in God.

The principle

The principle is to keep quoting the Word of God while you're pushing through, believing that God is going to do exceedingly, abundantly above all you can ask or think. Prosperity is always the result of obedience to God's principles.

The promise

When you learn the pattern and start applying the principle of worship, you become what I call a two-mile man in a one-mile world. The promise is your harvest. Harvest is the result of waiting long enough for God to bring to fruition what you've sown in faith.

> And Abraham stretched forth his hand, and took the knife to slay his son. And the angel of the LORD called unto him out of heaven, and said, Abraham, Abraham: and he said, Here am I.
>
> And he said, Lay not thine hand upon the lad, neither do thou any thing unto him: for now I know that thou fearest God, seeing thou hast not withheld thy son, thine only son from me.
>
> And Abraham lifted up his eyes, and looked, and behold behind him a ram caught in a thicket by his horns: and Abraham went and took the ram, and offered him up for a burnt offering in the stead of his son.
>
> —GENESIS 22:10–13, KJV

Abraham wasn't the kind of follower who just offered lip service to the Lord. He was more than an emotional Christian. Abraham was willing to take his God seriously enough to offer his promised son as his seed of worship. God isn't looking for us to kill our offspring to prove our love to Him. He's looking for those who are willing to obey His Word and worship no matter what.

"And he stretched forth his hand, and took the knife to slay him..." That's it! He was willing to go all the way. He was willing to journey up his mountain of worship. Abraham wasn't what we see every week in our services, a phony worshiper. Most Christians today can't even stay in services past noon. Most Christians only want God as someone who's going to keep them out of hell when they die. Not so with Abraham. He was willing to "take it to the mattresses." He was going to prove that he was in love with God more than he was in love with the promise. We will inevitably walk in all God's goodness when we can show Him that we love Him more than we love the harvest He provides.

How are we going to overcome drugs, alcohol or anything else that so easily entangles us? Why does it seem that people today have such a hard time getting free of what is keeping them in bondage? The reason is that most people today want God to do all the work to free them. They expect God to take away the desire. The truth is, the desire for what's holding you in captivity may not leave you for a long time. The power of deliverance is in the ability to fight your flesh. Submit to the pattern, start applying the principles, and you will receive the promise of freedom.

When we enter into this arena called life, we need to fight the curse of mediocrity. This curse has spread to epidemic proportions. Mediocrity is the quality or state of being mediocre. Mediocre means that you are "neither very good nor very bad; ordinary; average, not good enough, inferior..." Let me give you the Bible terminology: *lukewarm*. Revelation 3:16 says, "So then because thou art *lukewarm*, and neither cold nor hot, I will spue thee out of my mouth" (KJV, emphasis added).

Life is full of those who will never cross the line of mediocrity. The world is jam-packed with status-quo people who give up when the first sign of trouble shows. Not only is this epidemic plaguing the world, but it has also infiltrated the church. We are so full of people in our congregations who just want to clock their time and do nothing about making an impact. Most of us are people who can be so much more than average. In Christ Jesus we have been changed. We can do all things through Christ who strengthens us. The Word of God tells us that old things pass away and all things become new, yet we never seem to even get out of the pew!

It amazes me to look across the congregation and see so many of God's children looking as though they have just lost their best friend when they should be walking in victory. They just sit in the service and look around while others are trying to enter into praise and worship. They stare like someone who is lost and confused, as if they had died years ago but lack the good grace to lie down.

While I am watching them, I have this gnawing question in the back of my mind: *Will they ever get it?* Will they ever wake up and realize that there is more to Christianity than missing hell and making heaven? There is joy and unspeakable power...there is a walk of prosperity...there is an inner power greater than what they are facing externally.

Let's go deeper!

> You have heard that it was said, "Eye for eye, and tooth for tooth." But I tell you, Do not resist an evil person. If someone strikes you on the right cheek, turn to him the other also. And if someone wants to sue you and take your tunic, let him have your cloak as well. If someone forces you to go one mile, go with him two miles. Give to the one who asks you, and do not turn away from the one who wants to borrow from you.
>
> —MATTHEW 5:38–42

In the verses above I believe Jesus was saying that we, as believers, have within us the power to withstand the line of mediocrity...

How many of us can really explain Matthew 5:38–39?

Are you really going to let someone just walk up to you
and slap or punch your face without retaliation? I don't
really believe that this was what the Lord was trying to
get across to His disciples. There is a deeper meaning, and
I want to explain what I believe the Lord has revealed to
me in that regard.

God has put in every one of us an inner ability that is
greater than that of the enemy. There is more to us than
there is to them. When the enemy sends a trial or circumstance that would normally devastate others, it will not
destroy us. Disasters have a tendency to water down the
faith of most believers. The truth is, trials are sent to wear
us down, but when we understand the two-mile mentality, we will not enter into a spirit of desperation or depression. However, each of us will walk with the attitude that
there is more to me than what you can see. There's a
power in me that can survive the worst of tragedies.

Just look at all the people in New York and across
America who survived what happened on September 11,
2001. What the enemy assumed would have confused us
or dismantled us actually ignited unity and love in us for
one another. Out of the rubble and ashes of pain, death
and heartache, hoisted the spirit that has always been
seen in this great nation—the spirit of companionship, the
spirit of unity and the attitude that says, "No matter what
happens to Americans, there is more to us than what you
can see." This is the two-mile mentality. What the enemy
started, we will finish!

In the passage above, I believe the Lord is saying that
when the enemy takes your tunic, you should remember
that you also have a cloak to give. God will always supply
more than what your trial, your trouble, your enemy will
require...you have been filled with His power to move on
and to survive your trouble. If circumstances are slapping

your left cheek, you won't be destroyed because you have a right cheek. Just turn your head and move on. No need to try to fight what has already been whipped.

Because of what the Lord did on the cross, we can walk further than the one-mile line. We are more than conquerors! The one-mile line is the line of mediocrity. Only those who are willing to step over the one-mile line will accomplish great things.

CHAPTER 9

GiVinG WiLL PRODUCE FAVOR

I don't know what it is about money, but when I start talking about it or giving, no matter how energized the service is, the whole atmosphere becomes heavy with despair. Faces go from smiles to frowns, from joy to anger.

FAVOR KEY #13: FAVOR IS A SEED BEFORE IT'S A HARVEST

The majority of the congregation does not want to hear about giving, increase or harvest. The only explanation I can offer is this: I believe the people don't want to become accountable for what they hear.

There are people in the body of Christ who have never been taught the principles of giving. However, when you understand the law of increase and harvest...when you understand the power of a seed...you have become accountable for what you know. You are responsible of letting go of what you have in order to gain what God has.

Increase vs. harvest

I was in my sanctuary one day thanking God for giving me increase after I had sowed a faith seed. My wife and I sow seeds financially every week. We believe that instead of pleading about our financial situation, we should plant.

God changed our lives through the power of seed sowing five years ago. Since then we have experienced so much increase and blessings. I do not have the time to testify to them all, but here are a few!

- I have been driving a C 280 Mercedes for two years, and someone else is making the payment.

- I have been living in a 3,000-square-foot home, four bedrooms, three full-size bathrooms, an office and a garage for a year now, and God found a way to make the payments for the first twelve months.

- My wife and I have been on two cruises to Nassau, Bahamas, completely paid for—and not out of my pocket.

- Dr. Mike Murdock took my wife and me to the Holy Land free of charge—for us, that is.

- I had a $6,700 debt hanging over my head and someone completely paid off my debt...after I had let go of a $1,250 seed.

- I took in my wife's Mercedes to have some work done on it. The Lord impressed me to stay and talk to the manager of the dealership while I was waiting. While I was in his office, they called me from the Mercedes service shop to inform me how much the estimated fee was for my car repairs. There were seven payments left on the lease, and the estimate to fix my car was over $1,000. The manager told me to wait a minute, looked at my file, turned around and paid off my remaining lease. He then asked me if there was another Mercedes on the lot that my wife would

like to drive. My reply was that she liked the gray
E 320. The manager told me to come back in an
hour and take it. When we arrived back, he had all
the paperwork done. The only cost to me was the
next payment on the lease, which stayed the same
as the smaller Mercedes.

Favor "don't" make no sense. This list could go on for
pages. Someone is always handing me cash, buying my
meal or taking care of a trip. I'm so deep in the F.O.G.
(favor of God), the devil can't see me. It all started four
years ago when I began the work of sowing.

Not only has increase come in the way of financial favor,
but we have also experienced other forms of favor. My staff
at Living Word Fellowship has experienced the same
F.O.G. (favor of God).

Our youth pastor has been with me since he was a
teenager. He is now married and is working full time as our
youth pastor. His wife is our praise and worship leader. He
has experienced uncommon favor! Every year we have a
youth camp called Beach Invasion,* which I started in
1993. Each year we take one hundred to one hundred fifty
youths to Panama City, Florida, and turn them on to the
Holy Ghost. The whole purpose for this camp is to give
youth an experience with the supernatural power of God
instead of religion. Our motto has always been "every
youth goes"; money is no object. This commitment
requires us to walk in faith every year. This year we had
many youth go who could not afford to pay, but we stayed
true to our commitment that everyone goes. Money should
never be the reason we don't minister to someone. God

* If you would like information on Beach Invasion, please call us
  at (828) 325-4773 or write to Mind-set Youth Ministries, P. O.
  Box 3707, Hickory, NC 28603.

will take care of those who are willing to minister no matter the cost.

When the camp was over, we found ourselves in a deficit of $3,750, and our children's ministry was about to have their KIDS CAMP 2001 in two weeks. The deficit for the youth camp was holding up the ministry account for the kids' camp.

Both my youth pastor and children's pastor sat in my office asking me, "Pastor, what are we going to do?"

My reply was, *"Trust God!"*

Three days later, we were at a restaurant after our midweek service. God had really moved that night, and we were all charged up. I'm not going to only praise God after He demonstrates His favor...no way! I'm going to praise Him beforehand.

Someone walked up to my youth pastor and said, "We've been holding this check for a month, and we want to sow this into your youth ministry." The check was for *$20,000. Yes, you read that right!*

GET READY! FOR THIS IS ONLY INCREASE... WAIT TILL OUR HARVEST SHOWS UP!

Increase is when we gain enough to feel relief for the moment. Harvest is so much bigger. When harvest comes, you must be able to eat from it, sow from it, save from it and take care of the needy from it. Harvest is much greater than increase. I'm expecting harvest to come! Our harvest is a result of our giving. No matter what the enemy tries to do to you, don't let him stop your planting.

Our church administrator received a Cadillac Sedan Deville completely paid for.

Get ready for your harvest to show up! Don't let religion and stinking thinking rob you of what's rightfully yours by spiritual birth. If you're not already paying your tithe and sowing seeds, start this week. Never enter your church service without your seed to sow. I preach and teach my people at LWF never to enter the presence of God without your offering.

Everybody is getting excited about increase, but what about harvest? I was walking around my yard one day praising God about my increase and all the things God has done for me. All of a sudden I felt a quickening in my spirit. The Lord spoke to my heart and said, "You're getting excited about your increase...increase is not your harvest. When you sow a $100 and receive $1,000 for sowing, that's not your harvest, it's your increase. Harvest is much greater than increase." Harvest must be big enough to save out of, pay your bills out of and bless others out of.

Giving Will Produce the F.⊙.G.
(Favor of God)

Now there was a famine in the land—besides the earlier famine of Abraham's time—and Isaac went to Abimelech king of the Philistines in Gerar. The LORD appeared to Isaac and said, "Do not go down to Egypt; live in the land where I tell you to live. Stay in this land for a while, and I will be with you and will bless you. For to you and your descendants I will give all these lands and will confirm the oath I swore to your father Abraham. I will make your descendants as numerous as the stars in the sky and will give them all these lands, and through your offspring all nations on earth will be blessed, because Abraham obeyed me and kept my requirements, my commands, my decrees and my laws." So Isaac stayed in Gerar.

—Genesis 26:1–6

Isaac planted crops in that land and the same year reaped a hundredfold, because the LORD blessed him. The man became rich, and his wealth continued to grow until he became very wealthy. He had so many flocks and herds and servants that the Philistines envied him.

—GENESIS 26:12–14

Notice that Isaac planted while there was back-to-back famine in the land. That same year he reaped a hundred-fold because the Lord blessed him. That sounds good to me! The man became rich, and his wealth continued to grow until he became very wealthy!

Being wealthy is when you can keep what you have without doing what you did to get it all over again. Riches is what you have; wealth is what you are.

Harvest is what the church needs to be seeking, not just increase. Even Jesus said to pray to the Lord of the harvest…not to the Lord of increase. Giving with the expectancy of harvest is much more focused on others than increase is. Increase is just enough to feel a present lifting of my load. Harvest will not only lift my load, but also the loads of those around me.

*Love people, use things;
don't love things
and use people!*

We must learn to let go of what is in our hands. We must understand that there is nothing we have that God didn't give to us. If He wanted it, He could take it, but He's asking us to be givers so that we won't let what we have own us; we will own what we have.

Too many Christians are in love with things. Things become our idols when we focus on them instead of God. God wants us to love people and use things. Instead, we love things and use people.

Sometimes we wonder why there is not a lot of material wealth in the body of Christ. We can't handle it! God is a God of provision. The first and last miracles of Elijah were provisional, the first and last miracles of Elisha were provisional, and the first and last miracles of Jesus were provisional. The whole purpose of God sending His Son, Jesus, was to provide for us. God is *into* our harvest. He wants us to be blessed so we can be a blessing. Giving is the key to harvest, and sowing is the tool. Seeds aren't just limited to money. A smile, a kind gesture, a welcomed handshake—these are all seeds.

- Sow love; reap love!
- Sow kindness; reap kindness!
- Sow help; reap help!
- *Sow money; reap money!*

Give, and *it will be given to you*. A good measure, pressed down, shaken together and running over, will be poured into your lap. For with the measure you use, it will be measured to you.
—LUKE 6:38, EMPHASIS ADDED

Notice that *it will* be given to you. What will? Whatever you have given will come back to you, pressed down and running over.

The faithfulness of God is hinged on so many aspects of our walk with Him. We must learn to understand that there will never be a day in our lives when we can say, "I have arrived." We are all in spiritual process, being changed from glory to glory. Giving is one area that is overlooked in the body of Christ. Satan wants to keep us broke, busted and poor. We will never be able to afford to take the gospel beyond our own boundaries as long as we can't pay our bills. Let us become financially liberated, and we will affect the whole city, state and nation with our wealth.

LEARN TO LET GO AND LET GOD!

When I speak about giving, I don't mean just the tithe. Tithing is not giving. The tithe is not seed; rather, the tithe is *payment*. We are commanded by the Lord to *pay* our tithe. A tithe is 10 percent of what comes into your hand. There seems to be a lot of misunderstanding in the body of Christ about paying tithes. For some reason believers have watered down the responsibility of paying their tithe.

When we learn the biblical principles of tithing and giving, we will break out into so much abundance that others will be taken care of through it.

Jesus came to change our season! Before Jesus entered my life I was living in the season of drought and despair. When I accepted Him as Lord and Savior, my whole outlook changed. Jesus took me from shallow waters to deep waters. *Would you love to walk out of shallow water living? Do you desire to allow God to change your season and for you to live a life with no more dry seasons?* If you desire to see and experience the F.O.G. (faithfulness of God), learn to tithe, sow and be completely obedient to the Word of God.

We will become blessed when we give what we have to support the kingdom of God!

In Luke 5 we see this principle in action.

> And it came to pass, that, as the people pressed upon him to hear the word of God, he stood by the lake of Gennesaret, and saw two ships standing by the lake: but the fishermen were gone out of them, and were washing their nets. And he entered into one of the ships, which was Simon's, and prayed him that he would thrust out a little from the land. And he sat down, and taught the people out of the ship. Now

when he had left speaking, he said unto Simon, Launch out into the deep, and let down your nets for a draught.

And Simon answering said unto him, Master, we have toiled all the night, and have taken nothing: nevertheless at thy word I will let down the net. And when they had this done, they inclosed a great multitude of fishes: and their net brake. And they beckoned unto their partners, which were in the other ship, that they should come and help them. And they came, and filled both the ships, so that they began to sink.

When Simon Peter saw it, he fell down at Jesus' knees, saying, Depart from me; for I am a sinful man, O Lord. For he was astonished, and all that were with him, at the draught of the fishes, which they had taken.

—Luke 5:1–9, kjv

The Lord asked Simon if He could use his boat so He could teach the people about the kingdom. Peter had toiled all night fishing, and fishing isn't an easy job. He must have been exhausted. He had been working a physical job all night, casting and pulling nets, coming home with no rewards for his hard work. *What a day it was becoming!* After all of his hard work, Jesus required the assistance of his boat, and with that assistance came more hours of no sleep. Peter had to sit on the boat and listen to the preaching of the long-winded man of God.

Jesus finished His teaching, looked down at Simon and said, "Launch out into the deep, and let down your nets for a draught." The Amplified Bible says, "When He had stopped speaking, He said to Simon (Peter), Put out into the deep [water], and lower your nets for a haul."

The Lord was changing Simon's season from shallow-water fishing to deep-water fishing. Imagine what was going through the mind of Simon: *This Man is a teacher, He was raised a carpenter, and now He's going to instruct me on how to fish. Doesn't Jesus realize that I have stayed up all night fishing? My nets are already clean and put up for the day, and my family is already expecting me to be home. He wants me to go out into deeper waters and lower my nets. I can't believe this!* Oh yes, that's right…God was about to change his season, and change required something on his part.

Watch what Simon says next! "Master, we have toiled all the night, and have taken nothing: nevertheless at thy word I will let down the net."

Nevertheless at thy word I will let down my net.

The Amplified Bible says, "But on the ground of Your word, I will lower the nets [again]."

Simon Peter wasn't letting down his nets because he wanted to…

He wasn't letting down his nets because he believed he was going to catch something…

He wasn't even doing it because he had faith or expectation of blessing…

No, Simon said, "On Your word alone am I going to obey. Because of who You are. Lord, my obedience is not on what I'm feeling, but on what You're saying!"

When Peter obeyed, the blessing came.

> And when they had this done, they inclosed a great multitude of fishes: and their net brake. And they beckoned unto their partners, which were in the other ship, that they should come and help them. And they came, and filled both the ships, so that they began to sink.
>
> —LUKE 5:6–7, KJV

There was so much of a blessing that Simon had to call his partner. There was so much that the catch almost sank both their ships. Simon gave his ship and his time for the man of God to use. When Jesus was done with kingdom business, He blessed the *man who gave!* God is faithful to those who learn the power of giving, or should I say, sowing a seed. One more thing! Peter also fell down to his knees, repented, accepted the man of God and was chosen at that time to be one of His disciples.

It's only at the end of your obedience that you will discover your miracle.

Favor always follows obedience. Favor will come to you after you have proven your obedience to God's Word. If you divide the word *obedience* into three parts, the middle word would be *die*: OBE–*DIE*–ENCE.

You must be willing to die to your flesh to be a completely obedient believer. The more flesh you kill, the more obedient you will become. Obedience is the qualifier to favor and to God's faithfulness. You must be an obedient giver to be a good giver.

If You Want to Increase Your Living, Increase Your Giving

Conquering debt will produce the F.O.G. You aren't truly free until you are debt free. Giving is the best way to increase your storehouse. You can't just be a good giver in your church and not pay your bills at home.

The worst thing a believer can do is lag behind on his bills. We all have times of famine and have sown in times of lack. However, this shouldn't be the norm. If you are sowing what you owe others, stop! Pay your bills first, and be faithful to give what you have to the kingdom of God. Don't sow what belongs to others. Sow what belongs to you. Now, this isn't a popular thing to say, but I believe that when you get your life in order, your finances will begin to turn around. You may start out small, but you will finish *big*!

For example, let's say that your power bill is $150, and all you have in your checking account is $200. Pay your full power bill. Don't cut into what it will cost you to pay your power bill unless you are absolutely sure you have heard from God. If God is asking you to make an exception and prompting you to sow, sow at your level of sacrifice, then you will have the money to pay your power bill by the due date.

Let me impress a caution. Be very careful not to let someone stir you up and in the process forget your responsibility to your own commitments. I do not believe that God will impress on you to sow if it will cause your reputation to be stained.

Don't misunderstand me; *I'm not saying don't sow...* I'm saying use wisdom and discernment. Know how and when to sow. Learn to sow continuously...sow often... sow every time you're in an anointed service. Just learn to sow at your level and not at the level of others. If we would learn to sow at our level, we would have abundance in our churches. However, the norm is that half of the church sows, and the remaining are freeloaders. To sow at your level means sowing what you have, not your power bill money or your rent money.

Five years ago my wife and I started learning the principle of prosperity and that being blessed is to be a blessing. We started sowing seeds weekly in our church. At that time we were under a lot of debt, so the amount we sowed was a whopping ten dollars a week. At that season of our lives ten dollars was a sacrifice. Now we sow fifty dollars a week or more above our tithes. We can't wait until we are sowing one hundred dollars a week, and then five hundred dollars, and so on.

Learn to sow something! If all you have is one dollar, sow it! It would do more for you in the soil of your faith than in your pocket.

Don't overdo it, but don't "underdo" it either. Learn to stretch yourself, but also make sure your bills are being paid on time. When we put money in its proper place, we won't have to work for money; money will work for us. Money is a tool, and tools are supposed to be used. When a tool breaks, we get another one. Money was preordained to be used, not worshiped! Money was to take care of our needs, not to be sought after with all our might forty to fifty hours a week. Let's shout it right now, *"Money cometh to my house! I will get my finances in order."*[1]

God loves it when we are trying to get our house in order. He is very attentive to our desire to better ourselves, and He is pleased when we make the necessary efforts to do so. God will get involved with those who desire change. One of the largest setbacks in the body of Christ is *bad credit* and *slow bill payers.* My administrator told me that while he was in the financing business, every so-called Christian that borrowed money from his company never paid it back or filed bankruptcy. That is disastrous to the reputation of God—and to us.

Let's change that stigma by starting today with a heart of repentance. Our character and integrity are on the line. If you can't buy it, don't charge it for the minimum payment of ten dollars a month for the next ten to twenty years on a high-interest-rate credit card. That is illogical. Wait until you have the funds for what you want, and learn to trust God.

Debt is a curse, and we must break it. The line is drawn here today as you are reading this book and desiring to produce the *F.O.G. (favor of God).* Stop the insanity of debt! Start today; make a budget and stick to it. Start

paying off those high-percentage credit cards and loans. I
assure you that if you start, you will see God's participa-
tion in your life, finances and family. Money will start
showing up unexpectedly at your dwelling. When God
sees that you desire to become debt free, when He can
trust you to seek to free up others with your freedom, He
will begin to pour out His power and wisdom.

Let me give you a financial priority list:

1. Tithe
2. Sow
3. Bills
4. Savings
5. Yourself
6. Others
7. Retirement or investments

You cannot, and will not, have financial power until
you are *debt free*. How can we help others if we are barely
getting by ourselves?

Conquering debt will produce the *F.O.G.*

Unfortunately, this is not an exhaustive study on
finances. If you really desire to change your financial
future, then take time to study what financial leaders are
saying. Go to your local bookstore and inquire about
books on budgets, investments and good stewardship.

We can't change just because we have the desire to. We
must make the necessary effort.

At the end of your obedience is God's favor!

---

[1]Leroy Thompson, *Money Cometh: To the Body of Christ*
(Tulsa, OK: Harrison House, 1999).

CHAPTER 10

SEVEN ENEMIES THAT WILL STOP YOUR FAVOR

Favor is one of God's greatest gifts to mankind. Favor is something that we all can walk in, but none of us really deserve it. God chose to give us favor so that we can live blessed outside our natural means. God is our source of favor.

If you have read faithfully up to this part, then you should understand that favor is about to explode in your life. Let me instruct you right now to protect your favor. Never let those around you steal or rob you of it. If you are allowed access, don't feel bad if your friends aren't. Favor isn't fair! Too often we will start being favored by someone who can stretch us to the next level, but because we refuse to go along, we jeopardize our access to the favor of God. We let our feelings get in the way of our favor. In truth, if we would allow our growth and take the necessary steps to get to the next level, eventually all those who helped us, encouraged us and cheered us on would reap the benefit of our access.

When those around you start becoming jealous of your favor, they are not really for you. When you start growing or changing, you start reminding them they aren't. Dr. Murdock says that there are those who are around you that you should move away from you. The reason you are not growing or increasing is that God isn't going to release your harvest because those around you don't qualify. So, in reality, it's not *what* is on your ship, but *who* is on your ship that is stopping your increase! (See Jonah 1:4–10.)

When the wrong people are around you, wrong things will happen. You can have the right man placed around the wrong people, and he will never accomplish what he could have if he was placed around the right people.

Others matter in your life. Others can make you or break you. Hire the wrong staff, and you will be damaged in time. The favor of God is something I will never trade for people. Protect your favor!

Connection Is Important

Connection is important. *Who you are connected to, you will eventually become.*

There should be three connections taking place in your life.

1. You should be connected to a mentor who is teaching you and speaking instructions of change into you. This connection is one that you reach for. It's the connection that pulls you to a higher level.

2. You should be connected to your peers. This is the level of equality—those who are at the same level with whom you will hang out, fellowship or go to movies or other activities. Caution: Never assume that when you are in your mentor's atmosphere that you are equal. You are not just engaging in fellowship when you are with those who are

higher than you. You are to be instructed
and taught by them.

3. You should be connected with those whom
you are mentoring. This is your ability to
empty what has been put into you to influence others and make a difference in their
lives. These are the men or women who look
up to you.

A Change of Mind

When the children of Israel were about to enter into a
new level in their journey, God tried to change their
mentality while taking them through the wilderness. In
the first part of their journey they were just leaving slavery, and they had a slavery mentality. Then instead of
changing their mind-set and taking their place once more
as the children of promise, they traded in their slave
mentality for a welfare mentality. As long as God was
taking care of the bill and making sure they had no wants
or needs, the children of Israel were happy. The minute
crisis showed up, their disposition went sour. They were
not people of praise. They were people of complaints, and
they had no problem with letting everyone around them
know what they didn't like about their current situation.
They were "crisis-led." Let me throw a phrase at you:
"crisis-addicted."

There are people who can never live a day without a
crisis. They actually need the crisis they are in to give
them some form of focus. The problem with these kinds
of people is that they are never focused on the right
things. They are led by what's bothering them that day.
Whatever problem they are in, that is their current focus.
They will never go anywhere in life because they will

always be led by what's got them at the moment.

We are actually allowing our days to be filled with stress, heartache and failure when we let our circumstances dictate to us how we are going to set up our daily routine. Crises come and go. Learn to set up your day by what is priority instead of what is bothering you. You control your day, or circumstances will control you.

The children of Israel had come to the next place in their journey; they had now ended their forty years of wandering the wilderness and living solely at the hand of God's provision.

> For the land which you go to possess is not like the land of Egypt from which you have come, where you sowed your seed and watered it by foot, as a vegetable garden; but the land which you cross over to possess is a land of hills and valleys, which drinks water from the rain of heaven, a land for which the LORD your God cares; the eyes of the LORD your God are always on it, from the beginning of the year to the very end of the year.
>
> —DEUTERONOMY 11:10–12, NKJV

This land they were about to enter was a land that would cost them. They had to develop a new mentality so that if they dared to enter they must dare to conquer. They were moving from welfare into warfare! The Lord was saying to them, *"Up till now the meals have been on Me; the next meal will be on you."* The Bible says after they had crossed over, *"That day the manna stopped."* For any of us to walk in favor, we are going to have to understand that the good things in life really aren't free. There is a cost we must pay to walk in the favor of God, but we are going to have to learn that favor is a gift...a gift that needs to be protected *at all cost*. The truth is, all of us have enemies.

The Bible calls us conquerors, therefore we must have an opponent to conquer. When we are moving forward in faith, we are moving against resistance.

I know that when I said the word *enemies*, a hint of fear tried to creep into your spirit. Don't let fear enter. We need to understand that having an enemy isn't bad. Actually, it is necessary for you and me to be opposed in order for us to be conquerors. Our blessings are hinged on our victories. When we conquer, *we authorize our acceptance of the spoils*. Let me add this: You will not be rewarded for the enemies you face; you will only be rewarded for the ones you conquer. Everybody faced Goliath, but it was David who conquered him; therefore, it was David who got to take the spoils. Begin to view your enemy as your doorway to favor and prosperity. The enemy that you're begging God to take away might actually be the problem He sent. The enemy is the doorway to your harvest.

Read the next verses slowly.

> When the LORD your God brings you into the land you are entering to possess and drives out before you many nations—the Hittites, Girgashites, Amorites, Canaanites, Perizzites, Hivites and Jebusites, seven nations larger and stronger than you—and when the LORD your God has delivered them over to you and you have defeated them, then you must destroy them totally. Make no treaty with them, and show them no mercy...This is what you are to do to them: Break down their altars, smash their sacred stones, cut down their Asherah poles and burn their idols in the fire. For you are a people holy to the LORD your God. The LORD your God has chosen you out of all the peoples on the face of the earth to be his people, his treasured possession. The LORD did not set his affection on you and choose you because you were more numerous

than other peoples, for you were the fewest of all peoples. But it was because the LORD loved you and kept the oath he swore to your forefathers that he brought you out with a mighty hand and redeemed you from the land of slavery, from the power of Pharaoh king of Egypt. Know therefore that the LORD your God is God; he is the faithful God, keeping his covenant of love to a thousand generations of those who love him and keep his commands.

—DEUTERONOMY 7:1–9

Notice that the Lord names seven enemies that the children of Israel must conquer. There were more than seven nations in the land of Canaan, but God didn't command them to fight everyone…only seven of them. Real maturity isn't fighting everyone; it's having the discernment to know who to fight and who not to fight. God knew that if His people would conquer these nations, the others would surrender. When we walk according to the plans and purposes of God, we will not have to put forth the same effort as others do to achieve the same results.

FAVOR KEY #14: FAVOR IS KNOWING WHEN TO FIGHT AND WHEN NOT TO FIGHT

If you look closely at these seven nations, you will discover that there is a deeper message than just the fact that the children of Israel conquered them. I believe these enemies still exist today and that they are set up against the body of Christ to keep us from moving into our favor.

Remember God's instructions:

And when the LORD your God has delivered them over to you and you have defeated them, then you must destroy them totally. Make no treaty with

them, and show them no mercy...This is what you
are to do to them: Break down their altars, smash
their sacred stones, cut down their Asherah poles and
burn their idols in the fire.

—DEUTERONOMY 7:2, 5

It appears that God is not being very merciful. A closer
look at why He commanded such action will bring clarity
to God's instruction. You must conquer them, utterly
destroy them and completely annihilate them. Wipe
them off the face of the earth. Make no treaty with them;
show them no mercy.

God knew that if they were allowed to mingle with
His children they would eventually turn them to their
idol worship. They would marry their children and water
down His bloodline of promise.

When you see what these nations really stand for, you
will begin to understand why you must learn the art of
warfare! Warfare isn't what people desire to do. It is always
the result of having to be trained and pushed into conflict.
Most people don't wake up looking to go to war, but the
truth is, we are at war. We must recognize the necessity of
having a warfare mentality every day. In the Old
Testament, they fought this battle more in the physical
realm. As a New Testament believer our fight will have to
be won in the spiritual as well as the physical.

The first nation was the *Hittites*. In the Hebrew we will
discover that the meaning of the name *Hittites* is *"spirit of
terror or fear."*

Fear will be the first enemy you and I will have to
conquer.

Fear is the opposite of faith...you can never walk by
faith if fear is present. Fear will cause you to change your
focus...fear will paralyze your giving...fear will paralyze

your attempts to move past things that hurt you. I've counseled many people during my twenty-two years of ministry, and it never ceases to amaze me how many people stay in their current problems all because they are afraid to step out. Their fears dictate to them what they can and can't do. I couldn't stand to live my life always being afraid.

I can remember as a child growing up how fearful I was of the dark. I would lie in my bed at night and be totally afraid to look around my room for the sole fact that I might see the *"boogie man."* Now watch how fear works. The same room where I spent hours playing, drawing and creating my life's adventures in the daylight became my prison at night, and it was *all because of fear.* What was I afraid of? My belief of what was in the room when the lights were out. There was no *"boogie man."* There was never anything under my bed. The only thing I was afraid of was nothing more than what I had created in my own mind. My mind would create the movie that my spirit man would play out. When I matured, I learned that there's nothing to fear but fear itself.

Fear is created in our minds, not in our realities. When I make my problem bigger than my God, then I become afraid. But when I look at how big my God is, I start telling my problems to take a hike!

Fear will cause a father not to show affection to his children because of how he was treated as a child. Thus fear is opening the door of the past and hindering him from showing affection to his children in the present.

> For you did not receive a spirit that makes you a slave again to fear, but you received the Spirit of sonship. And by him we cry, "Abba, Father."
>
> —ROMANS 8:15

> For God hath not given us the spirit of fear; but of power, and of love, and of a sound mind.
>
> —2 Timothy 1:7, kjv

> There is no fear in love; but perfect love casteth out fear: because fear hath torment. He that feareth is not made perfect in love.
>
> —1 John 4:18, kjv

The first enemy you will have to face and conquer is the spirit of fear. Don't let this spirit stay around. Make no treaty with it, and don't compromise with it; in the spirit of the Lord take your knife of faith and stab this spirit and kill it.

What you refuse to conquer today will conquer you tomorrow.

The second enemy the children of Israel had to conquer was the *Girgashites*, which in the Hebrew means "one who turns back." It is the spirit of backsliding…someone who wants to go back or is always looking back.

You can never accomplish anything worth great value in life by constantly focusing on the past. Society is full of people who can never get past their last hurt, pain or problem.

Have you ever noticed these people? They never know what they have because what they've been through is always on their mind.

We have a windshield and a rearview mirror on our automobiles. Notice that the windshield is larger than the rearview mirror. The manufacturer of your vehicle wanted you to spend more time looking where you were going instead of where you came from. The rearview mirror serves as a reminder of what's behind you. Its purpose is for you to glance every now and then to see if something may have crept up behind you without notice. It was never the intention of the manufacturer for you to focus your entire attention on the rearview mirror.

When you are driving, your focus is set on where you are going, not where you've been. In the same respect, God knew that the children of Israel needed to focus on what was ahead of them, not what was behind them. Time after time the people of God would prove that they couldn't get the place from which they came out of their heads, and it cost them greatly.

> And Jesus said unto him, No man, having put his hand to the plough, *and looking back,* is fit for the kingdom of God.
>
> —LUKE 9:62, KJV, EMPHASIS ADDED

We have adopted a weak understanding of spiritual warfare. We believe that for us to be in warfare we must be fighting demons or evil spirits. In reality, warfare is fighting against anything that would try to stop you from getting what God has promised you. Your enemy wants to keep you in your past so that you won't take advantage of your present, and then he can rob you of your future.

When you are always looking back, you are letting your real desires be made known. *What you're looking at is mastering you!*

> On that day no one who is on the roof of his house, with his goods inside, should go down to get them. Likewise, no one in the field should go back for anything. Remember Lot's wife!
>
> —LUKE 17:31–32

Lot's wife was turned into a pillar of salt because her heart was still in Sodom. She really never changed her desires, so God dried her up. There are many believers in the church today who lift dried up hands in praise and

give dried up offerings, all because they still love the
world. They have never really changed their focus.

> But my righteous one will live by faith. And if he
> shrinks back, I will not be pleased with him.
>
> —Hebrews 10:38

> But when he asks, he must believe and not doubt,
> because he who doubts is like a wave of the sea,
> blown and tossed by the wind. That man should not
> think he will receive anything from the Lord; he is a
> double-minded man, unstable in all he does.
>
> —James 1:6–8

To doubt is to have faith in your adversary! Faith is
confidence in God.

Favor will take you anywhere but backwards!

Pray this prayer right now if you're willing to face and
conquer this enemy:

> *Lord, I confess that I have allowed the spirit
> of compromise to enter my life. I have been
> consumed with my own obsessions, and in the
> process have gone backward and not forward
> for You.*
>
> *Forgive me of my pride and selfish spirit. I
> openly confess and destroy any spirit that
> causes me to lose my focus. I will become
> obsessed with You, O Lord.*
>
> *In Jesus' name, amen!*

The next nation we must face is the *Amorites*, which in
the Hebrew means "the spirit of Babel." Babel, or evil
communication, will always cause confusion.

Words matter. Words are powerful. The Bible declares
that life and death are in the power of the tongue. Words
can be doors, walls or bridges.

Your words need to be studied before they are spoken. When you see confusion in a marriage, in relationships or in your church, it is most likely the by-product of the spirit of Babel.

Negative words can destroy the momentum of any great movement. Words are more powerful than steel or stone. We used to sing a song as children when other kids would make fun of us, "Sticks and stones may break my bones, but words will never hurt me." Not true! Wounds that are inflicted by objects take weeks to heal, but wounds inflicted by words can take months, years and sometimes a lifetime to heal. Words spoken never die except as we defeat them.

God knew that evil communication would poison His people faster than anything else.

> The unfolding of your words gives light; it gives understanding to the simple.
>
> —PSALM 119:130

> The words of a man's mouth are deep waters, but the fountain of wisdom is a bubbling brook.
>
> —PROVERBS 18:4

> The words of a gossip are like choice morsels; they go down to a man's inmost parts.
>
> —PROVERBS 18:8

> The tongue that brings healing is a tree of life, but a deceitful tongue crushes the spirit.
>
> —PROVERBS 15:4

> A man of perverse heart does not prosper; he whose tongue is deceitful falls into trouble.
>
> —PROVERBS 17:20

> Even a fool is thought wise if he keeps silent, and
> discerning if he holds his tongue.
>
> —PROVERBS 17:28

> The tongue has the power of life and death, and
> those who love it will eat its fruit.
>
> —PROVERBS 18:21

> As a north wind brings rain, so a sly tongue brings
> angry looks.
>
> —PROVERBS 25:23

Words can open or close doors for you. Your words are
powerful tools that can help you gain access to what you
need.

In Mark 11:23 Jesus tells the disciples that if they
speak to the mountain of opposition and do not doubt in
the heart, but have faith, the mountain of opposition will
have to get up and move.

> That whosoever *shall say* unto this mountain, Be
> thou removed, and be thou cast into the sea; and
> shall *not doubt in his heart*, but shall believe that
> those things which he *saith shall* come to pass; he
> shall have whatsoever *he saith*. Therefore I say unto
> you, what things so ever ye desire, when ye pray,
> believe that ye receive them, and ye shall have them.
>
> —MARK 11:23–24, KJV, EMPHASIS ADDED

When you speak, you release what you believe into the
atmosphere. When we speak according to what has
already been spoken, we add agreement to it. The power
of agreement with God's Word makes things happen.
Don't let the spirit of Babel cause you to say things that
are detrimental to your harvest.

When your emotions are attacked through sickness or
emotional distress, don't allow your attitude to dip and, in

the process, cause you to say things you will have to live out. Hold your tongue. Let me reiterate: Words are doors, walls or bridges.

Think about this: Your seeds are damaged by what you say. You dig up your potential for a great harvest when you speak against what the Lord is doing out of anger or fear. Your harvest, your blessing and your victories are all hinged on your words. Use the weapon of words *for* you and not against you. You destroy your victories every time you speak against what God has said.

Not only do your words hurt *you*, but they can destroy *others* as well. One negative word can change a whole nation. When Moses sent out the twelve spies, only two of them had a good report. The other ten began to speak negative words about the promise and land. When the Israelites heard the negative words, they began to lose hope. When people lose hope, they begin to complain and grumble about what they had instead of speaking what they can have.

Kenneth Hagin used to say, "People can have what they say; the problem is, they keep saying what they have." Learn to speak faith words instead of defeated words. For example, when you go to purchase a car and you see one you like, but know at this time it is out of your budget, don't say words like, "I can't afford that…" or, "I will never be able to drive a car like that…" Say faith words like, "I'll be back! Not today, but tomorrow."

Remember, favor is a seed before it's a harvest. Start sowing for your desired harvest. If you want to increase your living, increase your giving.

Enemy number four is the *Canaanites*, which in the Hebrew is "a proud look, spirit of pride."

Pride is a very dangerous spirit. Pride goes before a fall. Pride focuses on your needs and on gaining what you desire at the expense of others. Pride has the "What about me?" attitude. "Why didn't anyone pick me?" "Why is he or she always getting to...?"

The whole reason Lucifer isn't leading the choir of angelic beings today is because of the spirit of pride. When we begin to perceive that we are better than the truth, we are operating in pride. When a person begins to believe his or her own fan mail, he or she is on a fast track to destruction.

God knew that pride would eventually pollute the whole nation if not destroyed.

Enemy number five is the *Perizzites*, which represent the "spirit of indecision." A "double mind" will cause you to hesitate, and hesitation may cause you to lose your victory. Hesitation is none other than disobedience.

One time I was in a church meeting where the Spirit of the Lord was moving so strongly through the speaker that I felt the Lord impress on me to walk up to the front while the speaker was ministering and plant a seed. I sat there for what seemed to be a long time trying to argue with the Lord. I let God know that I had no problem sowing the amount He had commanded me to sow, but to walk up in front of all those people...My hesitation cost me greatly. While I was hesitating, someone else went before me, and the spirit of giving hit the service. Now watch how my hesitation cost me. It cost me the harvest of starting a giving movement in a service. Hesitation is disobedience in disguise. Indecision has cost men their wealth. If you understand the "stock market," you know that hesitation can cause you to lose millions of dollars.

Indecision can cause arguments in relationships. How many times have you been out to eat with someone and neither of you could make up your mind where to eat? The question gets asked, "Where do you want to eat?" The answer, "It doesn't matter." So the suggestion is made, and all of a sudden you hear, "I don't want to go there." Indecision causes an argument, and both of you become frustrated.

Another name for this is "fence riders," people who can never make up their minds whom they are going to serve. Joshua brought Israel to the point of decision when he said:

> Choose for yourselves this day whom you will serve
> …But as for me and my household, we will serve the
> LORD.

—JOSHUA 24:15

Enemy number six—the *Hivites*, which in the Hebrew means "idol worship."

Anything you are drawn to in your hour of need is your God. Anything you draw from in your hour of need becomes your God. If you have to have an alcoholic drink every time you become stressed or smoke a cigarette every time your nerves have been heightened, those items have become idols to you.

An idol is something that causes you to put an image on God. Webster's dictionary defines *idol* as "an image of a god, used as an object or instrument of worship; in monotheistic belief, any heathen deity; any object of ardent or excessive devotion or admiration; a false notion or idea that causes errors in thinking or reasoning; anything that has no substance but can be seen, as an image in a mirror; any image or effigy; an impostor."

In the Book of Exodus, Aaron made a golden calf for the people of God—an image for the children of Israel to worship. Aaron was not trying to defame God. He was trying to give the people a god they could see and touch, a god they could understand.

> And all the people brake off the golden earrings,
> which were in their ears, and brought them unto
> Aaron. And he received them at their hand, and fash-
> ioned it with a graving tool, after he had made it a
> molten calf: and they said, These be thy gods, O
> Israel, which brought thee up out of the land of
> Egypt. And when Aaron saw it, he built an altar
> before it; and Aaron made proclamation, and said,
> Tomorrow is a feast to the LORD.
>
> —EXODUS 32:3–5, KJV

When we make an image of our god, we are actually
trying to put God on our level. This attempt to bring God
to our level causes us to lose the *supernatural*, thus
making it easier to be disobedient.

The Lord declared to His people that they should love
Him with all their hearts and that they should have no
other gods before Him.

You say, "But Bishop, I don't have any other gods but
God." Let me ask you something…Does your schedule
have your focus? Does your job have your attention more
than God? How about accessories for your car, your
house, your boat or anything else you have acquired in life
that holds your attention more than God? What about
your attendance in your local church? Are you so tired
every week that you can only make a few church activities a month? How about your midweek attendance? Has
it dropped off to never or every now and then?

Stop and think for a moment. Look around your
church. Take an inventory this Wednesday night. Notice
who never comes, and you will probably discover there is
a "Hivite" in their life. Maybe it's in yours, too!

What about your television? Don't tell me it isn't an
idol in your house. Why does everything in the house face
it? The average family spends fifty hours a week watching

television. That's more hours than the average person works in a week. Fifty hours a week...that's three thousand minutes. Three thousand minutes a week watching television...more than seven hours a day of television. That's fifty hours of rape, murder, sexuality, stealing, lying, extortion, anger, deception, fighting, divorce and destruction of what is wholesome and good. The American populace is addicted to shows that promote drugs, fornication and adultery. What about MTV and VH1? They show videos that are absolutely terrible for people to watch, flaunting the rich lifestyles of these stars. The world has no problem showing off wealth, but let someone like a Mike Murdock, a Benny Hinn, a T. D. Jakes or any other person of God who has gained financial status talk about their wealth, and they are crucified. *What hypocrites!*

Fifty hours a week watching television—and the average Christian can't pray or read the Word one hour a week. No wonder the church is fading and the world is increasing around us. We have let idols enter all around us. Let's stand, fight and win against this slithering, sneaky, sly spirit.

Enemy number seven is the *Jebusites*, which in Hebrew means "to trample, or polluted speech."

Three of these seven enemies have to do with the tongue. Most of our downfalls and failures come from what we say more than what we do. Before a person falls, he or she will probably speak it before it happens. As we begin to gain understanding and revelation of what the Lord desires for us as children of promise, we need to learn how to speak as children of promise.

Learn to speak faith words. Faith words are words that speak into your future and not about your circumstance. Faith words speak life, not death, over all your situations.

The truth is, we are all going to suffer hardship. We cannot escape trouble. Life is made up of good times and bad times. We can change our feelings to joy even in bad times when we learn the secret to faith speaking. We begin to take a look at what we are going through with the perspective of how the Lord sees it instead of how man sees it.

God knew that for the children of Israel to conquer and to progress to success in the new land, they would have to control what they said. Negative words not only destroy you, but they also destroy others. A word of criticism causes you and others around you to lose faith. Critics are everywhere. They walk around looking for those they can destroy with their negative attacks. When I'm looking to hang out with someone, I'm not looking for that one who always has something negative to say about everyone or everything. I'm looking for those who speak joy and faith into me, not doubt and defeat.

Again, words matter! Study them...speak them with caution! They are doors, walls or bridges.

CONCLUSION

F*avor* is a gift. When it is given, it makes no sense. Protect your favor. Thank God daily for it. Confess that you are favored.

Favor is not what you own or drive. It's not your savings or checking account or your investments. Favor is not money, and favor is not what you live in. Favor isn't attached to what you own. Favor is what you are.

You are highly favored...you are walking in favor. The F.O.G. is looking for you right now, and when it shows up, it will make no sense how fast it can promote you, bless you and connect you! Favor can do in a day what it took others to do in a lifetime.

Favor is moving toward you right now. Favor is God's best-kept secret. If you discover that you are blessed and highly favored, you will live the rest of your life in the expectation that God is about to show you favor.

I want to speak favor over your life, your home, your church, your ministry and your finances...FAVOR!

In the name of Jesus! Favor!
Walk in the F.O.G. zone every day of your life!

—FOGMAN

Favor Time

Get ready for the power of favor to increase everything you do. God is about to pour out His blessings on you and on those around you.

Enlarge your tents...enlarge your boundaries... increase your dreams. Get a dream that is bigger than you, and it will be a God-given dream. Grasp hold of this: When you are dreaming, dream a dream that only God could accomplish. We serve an awesome and big God. He is capable of fulfilling any dream we can come up with.

Favor will never make any sense. Don't try to figure out God. God will never be completely understood; just when you think you have Him figured out, He becomes bigger. I don't need a God who can do natural things. I can do natural things; I can accomplish natural things. I need a God who can do supernatural things.

Sometimes God Has to Bring You Out So He Can Bring You In

After faithfully sowing for an increase in my finances, I received a pay cut.

I didn't completely understand, but I was determined to trust God. One of my friends who worked for a local car dealership told me that they were hiring someone to schedule appointments for their service department. It wasn't exactly the job I was looking for, but it would get my foot in the door.

However, when I went for the interview, I was offered an assistant management position in the service department. The pay was almost double my former salary.

Praise God for His faithfulness!

—CARLEN LEWIS
HUDSON, NORTH CAROLINA

Delight yourself in the LORD, and he will give you the desires of your heart.

—PSALM 37:4

Since high school, I have believed God to supply the finances needed for me to attend college. One Wednesday night I forgot to bring my Bible to church. Someone had left a Bible in the seat in front of me, so I borrowed it. I felt the Holy Spirit leading me to leave a twenty-dollar bill in the Bible. At that time twenty dollars was a lot of money for me, but I did what the Holy Spirit said. Shortly after sowing the twenty dollars, I received a scholarship for $2000. I am now attending Appalachian State University, and I thank God for my hundredfold harvest!

—BETH MCKEMY
HICKORY, NORTH CAROLINA

NO MATTER WHAT THE DEVIL HAS STOLEN, HE WILL HAVE TO GIVE IT BACK!

During one of our church services, I felt led to sow my whole paycheck. You can imagine how hard it is to give one week's income, but obediently I gave it.

I have a son who is now twenty-five years old. His father quit paying child support when he was a child. After sowing my seed, I received a letter from the child support enforcement office asking me to call them immediately, and in January of 2002, I received a child support check for $1,938.48. No matter what

the devil has stolen, he will have to put it back!
—PASTOR SHERRY HICKS
LENOIR, NORTH CAROLINA

WHEN YOU LET GO OF WHAT YOU HAVE, GOD WILL LET GO OF WHAT HE HAS!

Our church held a wisdom conference in November of 2002. During one of the services I felt the Holy Spirit nudging me to sow a check I had just received for doing some graphic work. Since it was the holidays, and there wasn't any money left in my checking account, sowing the whole check was a stretch for me. While I was walking to the altar to sow, an usher in our church gave me another check. I decided to sow it too. I needed a big miracle, and I knew that God would do what He said He would do! The Holy Spirit spoke to Bishop Jerry to tell the congregation to sow into my life, and they would receive double. Pastor Maryann, Bishop's wife, was led to buy Christmas for my two young daughters, Faith and Grace. When I left the Lord's house, He had tripled what I came in with!
—PASTOR DARRYL MILLER
NEWTON, NORTH CAROLINA

GIVE, AND IT SHALL BE GIVEN, GOOD MEASURE, PRESSED DOWN, SHAKEN TOGETHER

My husband was diagnosed with lung cancer in February of 2002. He and I are both self-employed, and he didn't have any health insurance. When his treatment was finally over, we had over $100,000 in hospital debt. During our annual "Make the Devil Pay" conference, I sowed a seed of $300 into the man of God. This was a step of faith because I didn't even have the money in my checking account. I had to wait until the next week to write the check, but this didn't matter to me. I believed God's Word that when you give it shall be given back to you...good measure, pressed down and shaken together. In September of the same year the hospital informed my husband and I that our debt was completely wiped out, and we didn't have to pay them anything!

—DEE MERCER
HICKORY, NORTH CAROLINA

HE IS AN ON-TIME GOD!

At the end of August, my car finally broke down. I say finally because it had been in need of repair for quite some time, but I didn't have the finances to have it fixed. My wife and I had been under Bishop Jerry's ministry for almost a year, and in that year we had been faithful to pay our tithe and sow our seeds. About two weeks after I parked my car, my wife's parents called us from Florida. Her stepdad had some tools he wanted to give me for work, which I really needed, but he didn't just give me tools. He gave us a car, a 1990 Buick Riviera with only 34,000 miles on it. God is always right on time!

—PASTOR TIM PROPST
ICARD, NORTH CAROLINA

FAVOR SCRIPTURES

And Jesus grew in wisdom and stature, and in *favor* with God and men.

—LUKE 2:52

Continuing daily with one accord in the temple, and breaking bread from house to house, they ate the food with gladness and simplicity of heart, praising God and having *favor* with all the people. And the Lord added to the church daily those who were being saved.

—ACTS 2:46–47, NKJV

And delivered him out of all his troubles, and gave him *favor* and wisdom in the presence of Pharaoh, king of Egypt...

—ACTS 7:10, NKJV

For surely, O LORD, you bless the righteous,; you surround them with your *favor* as a shield.

—PSALM 5:12

Then you will win *favor* and a good name in the sight of God and man. Trust in the LORD with all your heart and lean not on your own understanding.

—PROVERBS 3:4–5

For whoever finds me finds life and receives *favor* from the LORD.

—PROVERBS: 8:35

He that diligently seeketh good procureth *favour*: but he that seeketh mischief, it shall come unto him.

—PROVERBS 11:27, KJV

A good man obtains *favor* from the LORD, but the LORD condemns a crafty man.

—PROVERBS 12:2

Fools make a mock at sin: but among the righteous there is *favour*…The king's *favour* is toward a wise servant: but his wrath is against him that causeth shame.

—PROVERBS 14:9, 35, KJV

In the light of the king's countenance is life; and his *favour* is as a cloud of the latter rain.

—PROVERBS 16:15, KJV

He who finds a wife finds what is good and receives *favor* from the LORD.

—PROVERBS 18:22

Many will intreat the *favour* of the prince: and every man is a friend to him that giveth gifts.

—PROVERBS 19:6, KJV

A king's rage is like the roar of a lion, but his *favor* is like dew on the grass.

—PROVERBS 19:12

A good name is rather to be chosen than great riches, and loving *favour* rather than silver and gold.

—PROVERBS 22:1, KJV

Foreigners will rebuild your walls, and their kings will serve you. Though in anger I struck you, in *favor* I will show you compassion.

—ISAIAH 60:10

DECISION TIME

MAY I INVITE YOU TO MAKE JESUS CHRIST THE LORD OF YOUR LIFE?

The Bible says, "That if you confess with your mouth the Lord Jesus and believe in your heart that God has raised Him from the dead, you will be saved. For with the heart one believes unto righteousness, and with the mouth confession is made unto salvation" (Rom. 10:9–10, NKJV).

Pray this prayer with me today:

Dear Jesus, I believe that You died for me and rose again on the third day. I confess to You that I am a sinner. I need Your love and forgiveness. Come into my life, forgive my sins and give me eternal life. I confess You now as my Lord. Thank You for my salvation! I will walk in Your peace and joy from this day forward. Amen!

Signed   _____

Date   _____

[Mail this page today to the address below.]

❑ Yes, Fogman! I made a decision to accept Christ as my personal Savior today. Please send me my free gift to help me with my journey.

Name   _____

Address   _____

City   _____

State   _____

Zip   _____

Phone   _____

Birth date   _____

To contact Bishop Grillo:

The Fog Zone Ministries
P.O. Box 3707
Hickory N.C. 28603
(828) 325-4773
Fax: (828) 325-4877
www.fogzone.net
E-mail: fogman@charter.net

We believe in the power of partnership. Everyone needs someone to partner with.

Your needs are important to us. Write us, and we will put you in our F.O.G. Prayer Book and pray for your needs. Let us hear from you when you have a spiritual need or are experiencing a conflict in your life.

Bishop Grillo and staff, please enter into the prayer of agreement with me for the following needs:

_____

_____

_____

_____

_____

_____

ABOUT THE AUTHOR

Bishop Jerry and Pastor Maryann Grillo's vision is to bring the body of Christ to a greater knowledge of God's love for them and to forge a greater awareness of His desire to bring blessing, increase and victory in every situation they face in today's world.

With this in mind, they founded Living Word Fellowship (LWF) in Hickory, North Carolina, in January 1995. LWF is a center for healing, restoration and revitalization for those looking for a God who is more than just a Savior, but Lord in every aspect of life.

Bishop Grillo spent fourteen years in youth ministry after completing his studies at Southeastern College in Lakeland, Florida, in 1986. Through circumstances early in his ministry, God planted into Bishop Grillo a deep burning to "glean the fields" and "harvest souls" that religion had discarded as unreachable and valueless. This has remained the focal point of his passion in ministry and the driving force of Living Word Fellowship. Since its inception, LWF has brought hope to the community by feeding, clothing and assisting many who are homeless, unemployed, uneducated, hungry and hurting. This is truly the reason Jesus came into the world.

Bishop Grillo holds a bachelor of arts in pastoral ministry from Christian Bible College and Seminary in Independence, Missouri, a masters in counseling and psychology, and a doctorate in Christian counseling from the same school.

He also is a member of the American Association of

Christian Counselors. He is founder and senior pastor of Living Word Fellowship, and founder of Break Forth Ministries International, a licensing body for churches and ministers. Bishop Grillo is also a board member of Dr. Mike Murdock's Wisdom Center.

Bishop Grillo is a well-known conference and motivational speaker. He has traveled locally and internationally, and he has authored five books.

Bishop Grillo and Pastor Maryann have been married since 1988 and have a son, Jerry III, and a daughter, Jordan.